MCPL - 15616 E. 24 HWY.
INDEPENDENCE, MO 64050

3001000371734 8

Hulick, Kathryn   520 H877
The night sky

AF081708

WITHDRAWN
FROM THE RECORDS OF THE
MID-CONTINENT PUBLIC LIBRARY

FIELD GUIDES FOR KIDS

THE NIGHT SKY

Kathryn Hulick

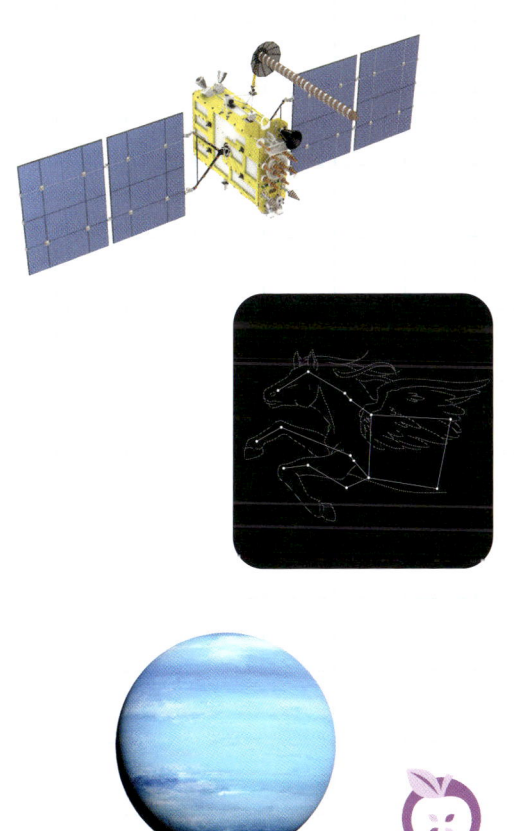

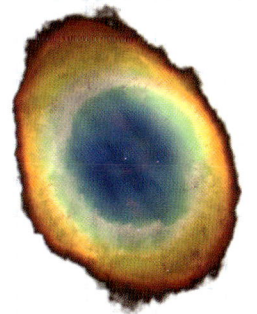

Abdo Reference

An Imprint of Abdo Publishing | abdobooks.com

CONTENTS

What Is the Night Sky? 4
How to Use This Book 6

The Solar System

Mercury 8
Venus 9
Mars 10
Ceres 11
Vesta 12
Jupiter 13
Saturn 14
Uranus 15
Neptune 16
Pluto 17

Moons

The Moon 18
Lunar Eclipse 19
Io 20
Europa 21
Ganymede 22
Callisto 23
Titan 24
Rhea 25

Constellations

Andromeda 26
Aquarius 27
Aquila 28
Aries 29
Boötes 30
Cancer 31
Canis Major 32
Capricornus 33
Cassiopeia 34
Centaurus 35
Cepheus 36
Cetus 37
Corona Borealis 38
Crux 39
Cygnus 40
Draco 41
Eridanus 42
Gemini 43
Hercules 44
Hydra 45
Leo 46
Libra 47
Lyra 48
Ophiuchus and Serpens 49
Orion 50
Pegasus 51
Perseus 52
Pisces 53
Sagittarius 54
Scorpius 55
Taurus 56
Ursa Major 57
Ursa Minor 58
Virgo 59

Stars

Aldebaran	60
Alpha Centauri	61
Antares	62
Arcturus	63
Betelgeuse	64
Canopus	65
Capella	66
Castor and Pollux	67
Deneb	68
Eta Carinae	69
Fomalhaut	70
Mizar and Alcor	71
Polaris	72
Procyon	73
Regulus	74
Rigel	75
Sirius	76
Vega	77

Star Clusters

Alpha Persei Moving Group	78
Beehive Cluster	79
Double Cluster	80
Hercules Globular Cluster	81
Hyades	82
Jewel Box	83
Omega Centauri Globular Cluster	84
Pleiades	85

Nebulae

Carina Nebula	86
Coalsack Nebula	87
Crab Nebula	88
Dumbbell Nebula	89
Eagle Nebula	90
Horsehead Nebula	91
Orion Nebula	92
Ring Nebula	93

Galaxies

Andromeda Galaxy	94
Large and Small Magellanic Clouds	95
The Milky Way	96
Whirlpool Galaxy	97

Comets

Halley's Comet	98
Future Bright Comets	99

Meteor Showers

Quadrantids	100
Perseids	101
Leonids	102
Geminids	103

Atmospheric Phenomena

The Northern and Southern Lights	104
Sprites	105

Human Objects

International Space Station	106
Satellites	107

Glossary	108
To Learn More	109
Photo Credits	110

WHAT IS THE NIGHT SKY?

The night sky inspires wonder and amazement in people of all ages. All major world cultures have told stories about the stars, planets, and Milky Way. Most grouped the stars together into shapes called constellations. Different cultures saw different shapes resembling people, animals, and objects. Astronomers today recognize 88 separate constellations in the night sky.

THE MOVING SKY

- During the course of a night, constellations appear to rotate around the sky. The timing of this rotation changes over the course of a year. New constellations become visible just after sunset, and other ones disappear beyond the horizon.

- The stars themselves aren't moving like this. Earth spins on its axis and orbits the sun. These motions change our view of the stars. Some constellations and night sky objects are visible only from the Northern Hemisphere. Others are visible only from the Southern Hemisphere.

- All of the objects in our solar system orbit around the sun. Most of them move along a nearly flat plane called the ecliptic. The sun follows the line of the ecliptic during the daytime. Planets move along this same path but are easiest to see at night.

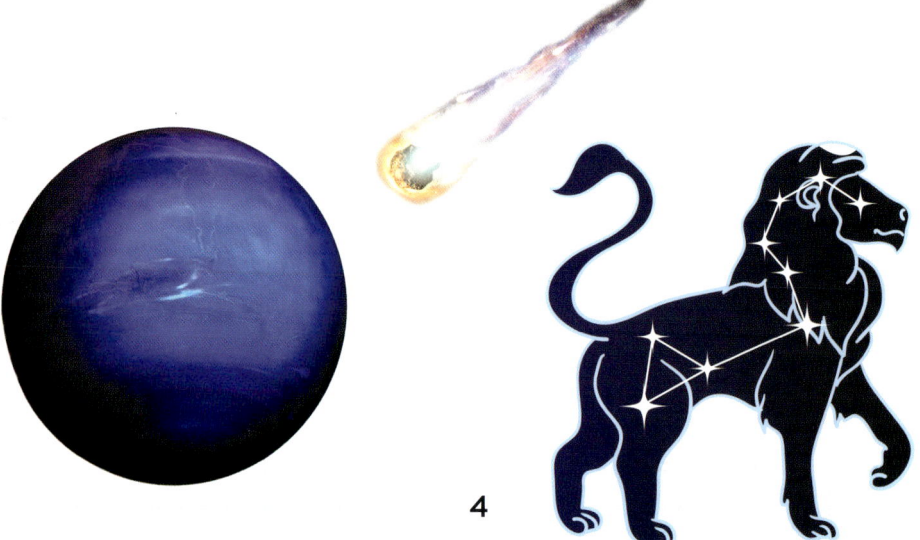

SEEING IN THE DARK

In the past, the night sky was clear and bright everywhere. But today artificial lights shining from homes, buildings, vehicles, and more cause light pollution. In cities and suburbs, light pollution washes out everything except the very brightest stars and planets. The best night sky viewing experiences are in dark rural areas. Most of the sights in this book are visible to the naked eye in a very dark sky. Binoculars or telescopes can provide more detail and bring dim objects into view.

Astronomers use a measurement called magnitude to tell how bright something appears in the sky. The scale goes from negative to positive. The lower the number, the brighter an object is. For example, the moon is the brightest thing in the night sky. Its magnitude is about -12.6. In a completely dark sky, most people can see things as dim as magnitude +6.0. Light pollution may limit visibility to magnitude +2.0 and brighter.

HOW TO USE THIS BOOK

Tab shows the night sky object category.

The night sky object's name appears here.

MOONS

IO

In 1610, Italian astronomer ... Jupiter through one of the world's first telescopes. With this tool, he saw four moons. Astronomers still call them the Galilean satellites. They are the largest of Jupiter's many moons. Io is one of these moons. It is the closest one to Jupiter. Volcanoes are scattered on Io's surface. Some spew lava as far as 250 miles (402 km) into space.

HOW TO SPOT

Where: Lined up with Jupiter
When: Whenever Jupiter is visible
... telescope
...: +5.0
...eter of
... (3,643 km)

How to Spot boxes explain where to find the night sky object and what it looks like.

The *Voyager 2* spacecraft took photos of volcanoes erupting on Io.

FUN FACT
Io is the only world other than Earth known to have active volcanoes.

Fun Facts give interesting information about night sky objects.

EUROPA

Europa is one of Jupiter's moons. It has a very smooth, shiny surface of ice that is several miles thick, crisscrossed with cracks and streaks. This icy world reflects lots of light, but binoculars or a telescope are required to see Europa because it is so close to Jupiter in the sky. Scientists have found evidence that a vast liquid ocean flows beneath Europa's surface. This moon has an atmosphere that contains oxygen, though not very much of it.

HOW TO SPOT

Where: Lined up with Jupiter
When: Whenever Jupiter is visible
How: Binoculars or a small telescope
Magnitude: +5.3
Size: Diameter of 1,940 miles (3,120 km)

LIFE BENEATH THE ICE?

Life thrives beneath ice in Earth's oceans. Some scientists think the subsurface ocean on Europa could be home to alien microbes. Searching for life there is one of NASA's top goals. It planned to launch the *Europa Clipper* spacecraft to study Europa's ocean.

THE SOLAR SYSTEM

MERCURY

Mercury, the closest planet to the sun, is named after the Roman god of messages and speed. It is the fastest planet in the solar system, zipping along at 29 miles per second (47 km/s). The sun's light usually hides this planet from view. But at certain times of the year, the planet is visible near the horizon just after sunset or just before sunrise. At its brightest, Mercury shines with a yellow-orange hue, more brightly than any star.

HOW TO SPOT

Where: Northern or Southern Hemisphere

When: Varies; use a sky chart to check

How: Naked eyes

Location: Very close to the horizon, near where the sun sets or rises

Distance from the Sun: 36 million miles (58 million km)

Magnitude: As bright as -1.9

Size: Diameter of 3,032 miles (4,880 km)

Special telescopes can be used to safely watch Mercury pass in front of the sun.

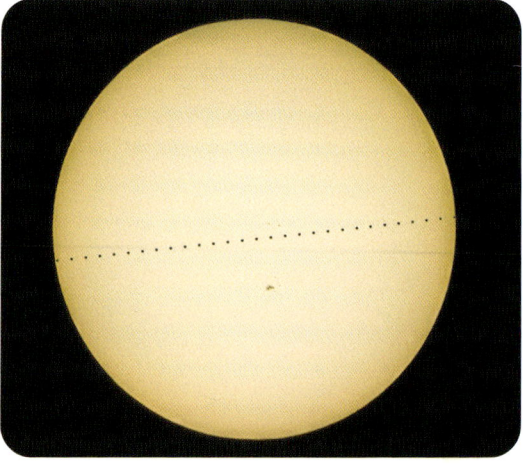

VENUS

Venus is the brightest planet in the night sky and the closest planet to Earth. It is often called the morning star or the evening star, since it rises and sets each day, just like the sun. This planet would not be pleasant to visit. It has a thick, heavy atmosphere filled with clouds of sulfuric acid, a chemical that burns skin and smells like rotten eggs. The temperature near the surface is hot enough to melt lead, and the air pressure would crush a submarine. The ancient Maya associated Venus with their most powerful god.

FUN FACT
Venus spins very slowly. Its day is longer than its year.

HOW TO SPOT

Where: Northern or Southern Hemisphere
When: For a few hours after sunset or before sunrise
How: Naked eyes
Location: Near the horizon where the sun sets or rises
Distance from the Sun: 67 million miles (108 million km)
Magnitude: As bright as -4.5
Size: Diameter of 7,520 miles (12,100 km)

THE SOLAR SYSTEM

MARS

Mars is often called the red planet. It looks orange or reddish from far away, but from the surface its sky is pink and the ground is mostly dark yellow. Mars is the only planet where humans have landed robotic rovers. In 2021, the NASA rovers *Curiosity* and *Perseverance* and the Chinese rover *Zhurong* were all studying the planet. Researchers have learned that billions of years ago, liquid water flowed on Mars. Now the planet is cold, dusty, and rocky, with almost no atmosphere.

HOW TO SPOT

Where: Northern or Southern Hemisphere
When: Varies; use a sky chart to check
How: Naked eyes
Location: Following the sun after it sets
Distance from the Sun: 142 million miles (229 million km)
Magnitude: As bright as -2.9
Size: Diameter of 4,212 miles (6,779 km)

FUN FACT
The largest volcano in the solar system, Olympus Mons, is located on Mars.

HUMANS ON MARS

Elon Musk, founder of the company SpaceX, plans to send humans to Mars. NASA, the US government space agency, has plans to get people there too. The trip will take six to nine months in each direction. It will be a risky journey. Mars has no breathable air, and it is colder than Antarctica.

CERES

Millions of rocky chunks called asteroids orbit in a band between Mars and Jupiter. This is called the asteroid belt. The asteroids here range in size from large boulders to miniature worlds. The largest of them is Ceres. In 2006, astronomers promoted it from an asteroid to a dwarf planet. Ceres contains lots of water, but most likely all of it is frozen. Viewing Ceres is very tricky since it moves from night to night and can be viewed only through binoculars or a telescope. Use online resources to locate it.

HOW TO SPOT

Where: Northern or Southern Hemisphere
When: Varies; use a sky chart to check
How: Binoculars or a telescope
Location: Varies; use online resources
Distance from the Sun: 257 million miles (414 million km)
Magnitude: As bright as +7.0
Size: Diameter of 592 miles (952 km)

The *Dawn* spacecraft arrived at Ceres in 2015.

THE SOLAR SYSTEM

VESTA

Vesta is the second-largest body in the asteroid belt between Mars and Jupiter. But it is the brightest because its shiny surface reflects more light than Ceres does. When Vesta travels closest to Earth, it may be visible to the naked eye in a very dark sky. Vesta doesn't qualify as a dwarf planet because it isn't quite large enough and its shape isn't quite spherical. However, scientists believe it has a planet-like structure with a core and crust. In Roman mythology, Vesta is the goddess of home and the hearth.

FUN FACT
Asteroids and comets sometimes smash into planets. In case astronomers spot one that could collide with Earth, engineers are thinking of ways they could knock it off course.

HOW TO SPOT

Where: Northern or Southern Hemisphere
When: Varies; use a sky chart to check
How: Binoculars
Location: Varies; use a sky chart to check
Distance from the Sun: 219 million miles (352 million km)
Magnitude: As bright as +5.1
Size: Diameter of 326 miles (525 km)

A close-up view of Vesta from the *Dawn* spacecraft

JUPITER

Jupiter, named for the king of the Roman gods, is the largest planet in the solar system. It has twice the mass of all the other planets combined. Seventy-nine moons orbit around the giant planet, and more will likely be discovered. Jupiter is made of layers of swirling gases surrounding a molten metal core. Jupiter's most famous feature is the Great Red Spot. This is a storm that is almost twice the size of Earth. The *Juno* spacecraft has been studying Jupiter and its moons since 2016.

HOW TO SPOT

Where: Northern or Southern Hemisphere

When: Varies; use a sky chart to check

How: Naked eyes

Location: In any one of the 12 zodiac constellations

Distance from the Sun: 484 million miles (779 million km)

Magnitude: -1.6 to -2.6

Size: Diameter of 88,846 miles (142,984 km)

FINDING THE PLANETS

The planets in our solar system are much closer to us than the stars we see in the night sky. This means that while the stars appear in consistent patterns, the planets move around throughout the year. There is no single place to find Jupiter or other planets in the night sky. However, the planets can be found near the 12 zodiac constellations. Ancient people noted that the planets remained near this line of constellations in the sky. This results from the fact that the objects in our solar system travel around the sun in a flat disc shape.

THE SOLAR SYSTEM

SATURN

Many people consider Saturn to be the most beautiful planet to observe because of its stunning rings, which are made of swirling pieces of rocks and ice. The rings are thousands of miles wide but just 30 feet (9 m) thick in some places. The spacecraft *Cassini* spent 13 years observing Saturn and its many moons. As a gas giant, Saturn has no solid ground. Its atmosphere is filled with swirling winds that blow harder than the strongest hurricane on Earth.

FUN FACT
Saturn has a very low density. It would float on water—if you could find a lake big enough to hold it.

HOW TO SPOT

Where: Northern or Southern Hemisphere
When: Varies; use a sky chart to check
How: Naked eyes (use a telescope to see the rings)
Location: In any one of the 12 zodiac constellations
Distance from the Sun: 886 million miles (1,426 million km)
Magnitude: +0.6 to +1.5
Size: Diameter of 72,367 miles (116,464 km)

URANUS

Uranus is the only sideways planet. As it travels around the sun, it spins on its side instead of spinning upright, as the other planets do. This means that seasons on Uranus last 20 Earth years or longer. The planet is icy and windy with a unique blue-green color and very faint rings. Ancient people didn't know about Uranus. William Herschel discovered the planet with a telescope in 1781. Most of Uranus's 27 moons are named after characters from William Shakespeare's works.

HOW TO SPOT

Where: Northern or Southern Hemisphere

When: Varies; use a sky chart to check

How: Binoculars

Location: In any one of the 12 zodiac constellations

Distance from the Sun: 1.8 billion miles (2.9 billion km)

Magnitude: +5.3

Size: Diameter of 31,518 miles (50,724 km)

A small telescope or binoculars can be used to see Uranus in the night sky.

THE SOLAR SYSTEM

NEPTUNE

Neptune is the solar system's farthest planet from the sun. It is bright blue in color and was named after the Roman god of the sea. In fact, Neptune is almost entirely an ocean, but instead of salt water it is made of a thick, slushy mixture of water, ammonia, and methane. Winds swirl in the atmosphere above, reaching speeds of 1,500 miles per hour (2,400 kmh). The planet has reddish rings and 14 moons. Its largest moon is Triton.

HOW TO SPOT

Where: Northern or Southern Hemisphere
When: Varies; use a sky chart to check
How: Small telescope
Location: In any one of the 12 zodiac constellations
Distance from the Sun: 2.8 billion miles (4.5 billion km)
Magnitude: +7.8
Size: Diameter of 30,599 miles (49,244 km)

The *Voyager 2* spacecraft launched from Earth in 1977. It reached Neptune in 1989.

PLUTO

Pluto is a small, rocky, frigid dwarf planet. Seeing this dim, distant world requires a large telescope. Clyde Tombaugh discovered Pluto in 1930. For decades, it was considered the ninth planet in the solar system. But then astronomers discovered that Pluto is just one of many icy objects that form a huge ring called the Kuiper Belt. Instead of adding more planets, in 2006 they decided to call Pluto a dwarf planet. Pluto follows a diagonal, stretched-out orbit. Occasionally, it comes closer to the sun than Neptune.

HOW TO SPOT

Where: Northern or Southern Hemisphere
When: Varies; use a sky chart to check
How: Large telescope
Location: Varies; use a sky chart to check
Distance from the Sun: 3.7 billion miles (5.9 billion km)
Magnitude: +13.6
Size: Diameter of 1,430 miles (2,302 km)

The *New Horizons* probe studied Pluto and Charon in 2015.

FUN FACT
Pluto's moon Charon is half Pluto's size. Together they are sometimes called a double dwarf planet system.

MOONS

THE MOON

Many cultures have revered the moon as a god or goddess, and it is still a beloved sight in the night sky. It is visible everywhere, even in places with a lot of light pollution. The moon appears to shine brightly, but in fact it is reflecting sunlight. As the moon orbits Earth, it reflects less sunlight and wanes, becoming thinner until it reaches the dark new moon phase. Then it waxes, becoming thicker until it is full again. This cycle takes approximately 29 days.

HOW TO SPOT

Where: Varies
When: Any night except during a new moon
How: Naked eyes
Distance: 238,855 miles (384,400 km) from Earth
Magnitude: -12.6
Size: Diameter of 2,159 miles (3,475 km)

MOON LANDINGS

The moon is the only place beyond Earth that humans have visited. Neil Armstrong and Buzz Aldrin set foot on the moon for the first time on July 20, 1969. On later visits, astronauts hit golf balls on the moon and drove a lunar rover.

LUNAR ECLIPSE

The moon orbits Earth on a tilted path. Usually, when the moon is on the opposite side of Earth from the sun, we see a full moon that shines brightly. But a few times each year, the sun, Earth, and moon line up just right, and Earth's shadow falls across the full moon. This is called a lunar eclipse. Some ancient Inca people believed that a lunar eclipse meant a jaguar was attacking the moon. They would make lots of noise to scare it away.

FUN FACT
The moon doesn't disappear from view during an eclipse. Instead, it appears red or orange.

HOW TO SPOT

Where: Varies; check NASA's website for locations
When: Usually twice each year; check NASA's website for dates
How: Naked eyes
Duration: Typically several hours

MOONS

IO

In 1610, Italian astronomer Galileo Galilei looked at Jupiter through one of the world's first telescopes. Using this tool, he saw four moons. Astronomers still call them the Galilean satellites. They are the largest of Jupiter's many moons. Io is one of these moons. It is the closest one to Jupiter. Volcanoes are scattered on Io's surface. Some spew lava as far as 250 miles (402 km) into space.

HOW TO SPOT

Where: Lined up with Jupiter
When: Whenever Jupiter is visible
How: Small telescope
Magnitude: +5.0
Size: Diameter of 2,264 miles (3,643 km)

The *Voyager 2* spacecraft took photos of volcanoes erupting on Io.

FUN FACT
Io is the only world other than Earth known to have active volcanoes.

EUROPA

Europa is one of Jupiter's moons. It has a very smooth, shiny surface of ice that is several miles thick, crisscrossed with cracks and streaks. This icy world reflects lots of light, but binoculars or a telescope are required to see Europa because it is so close to Jupiter in the sky. Scientists have found evidence that a vast liquid ocean flows beneath Europa's surface. This moon has an atmosphere that contains oxygen, though not very much of it.

HOW TO SPOT

Where: Lined up with Jupiter
When: Whenever Jupiter is visible
How: Binoculars or a small telescope
Magnitude: +5.3
Size: Diameter of 1,940 miles (3,120 km)

LIFE BENEATH THE ICE?

Life thrives beneath ice in Earth's oceans. Some scientists think the subsurface ocean on Europa could be home to alien microbes. Searching for life there is one of NASA's top goals. It planned to launch the *Europa Clipper* spacecraft to study Europa's ocean.

MOONS
GANYMEDE

Ganymede, another one of Jupiter's moons, is the largest moon in the solar system. It is bigger than the planet Mercury. Due to its large size, it can be viewed through binoculars. Ganymede is the only moon with a magnetic field. This field traps charged particles, creating glowing auroras at the moon's north and south poles, just like the northern and southern lights on Earth.

HOW TO SPOT

Where: Lined up with Jupiter
When: Whenever Jupiter is visible
How: Binoculars
Magnitude: +4.6
Size: Diameter of 3,270 miles (5,262 km)

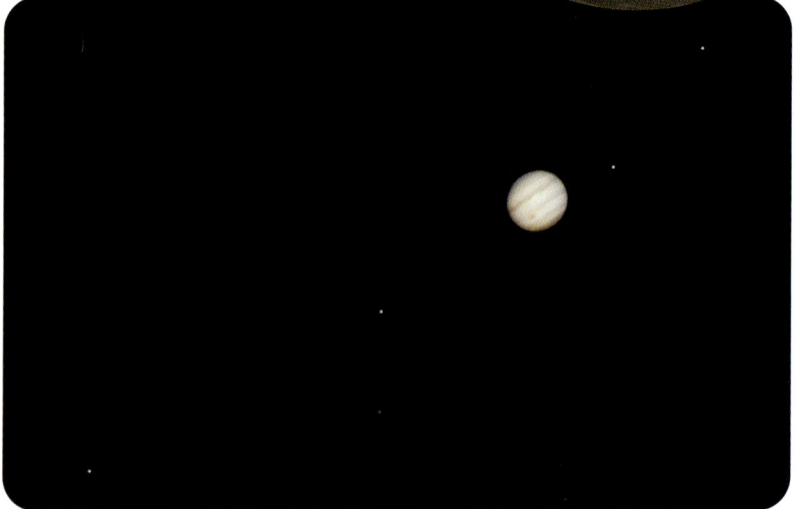

Jupiter's four largest moons, including Ganymede, can be seen through a telescope near the gas giant.

CALLISTO

Of the four Galilean moons, Callisto orbits the farthest from Jupiter. Its surface is speckled with many light spots. All of them are craters left behind after asteroids or comets struck the surface. In fact, this moon has more craters than any other object in the solar system. Its surface may be billions of years old.

HOW TO SPOT

Where: Lined up with Jupiter
When: Whenever Jupiter is visible
How: Binoculars
Magnitude: +5.7
Size: Diameter of 2,996 miles (4,821 km)

FUN FACT
Jupiter has dangerous radiation around it. Callisto's distance from the planet means the radiation is lower there, so experts believe it could be a good place for a future human base near Jupiter.

MOONS

TITAN

Saturn has 82 known moons, but only seven can be viewed from Earth through a typical telescope. Titan is the largest and easiest to observe. It's also the only moon in the solar system with a significant atmosphere. The yellow, hazy sky is filled with nitrogen and methane. The moon is so cold that methane and ethane, which are gases on Earth, are found in liquid form. The Dutch astronomer Christiaan Huygens discovered Titan in 1655 using a telescope. In 2005, the *Huygens* probe landed on Titan to study this moon.

Titan is larger than our moon but much smaller than Earth.

FUN FACT
Methane and ethane fall as rain and flow as rivers and lakes on Titan.

HOW TO SPOT

Where: Next to Saturn
When: Whenever Saturn is visible
How: Telescope
Magnitude: +8.5
Size: Diameter of 3,200 miles (5,149 km)

Scientists work on the *Huygens* probe in 1997.

RHEA

A good telescope can reveal six other moons of Saturn in addition to Titan. They are Rhea, Tethys, Enceladus, Iapetus, Dione, and Mimas. NASA describes Rhea, the second largest of Saturn's moons, as a "frozen, dirty snowball" because it is composed of ice and rock mixed together. Rhea is the only moon known to have a ring around it. In Greek mythology, Rhea was the mother of Zeus, king of the gods.

HOW TO SPOT

Where: Next to Saturn
When: Whenever Saturn is visible
How: Telescope
Magnitude: +10
Size: Diameter of 950 miles (1,528 km)

ENCELADUS

Enceladus is among Saturn's most interesting moons. Like several other moons, it most likely has a liquid ocean beneath its frozen surface. What make it unique are huge jets that spray this ocean out into space. The spacecraft *Cassini* grabbed samples of this spray. Scientists learned that this ocean has the chemical ingredients that might make life possible there.

CONSTELLATIONS

ANDROMEDA *(THE CHAINED MAIDEN)*

Andromeda belongs to a group of constellations that tell a story from Greek mythology. In the story, Andromeda's mother, Cassiopeia, angers the gods. The gods tell Cassiopeia's husband, Cepheus, to sacrifice their daughter to the sea monster Cetus. The hero Perseus arrives just in time on the winged horse Pegasus to save her. All these constellations are located in the same region of the sky. Andromeda can be difficult to see unless the sky is very dark.

HOW TO SPOT

Where: Best viewed from the Northern Hemisphere
When: Evening in October and November
How: Naked eyes
Location: Between Pegasus and Cassiopeia
Size: Medium

AQUARIUS *(THE WATER BEARER)*

Aquarius is a large but faint constellation representing a man pouring water from a jar. It is located in a section of sky known as the Sea, which is home to several other water-themed constellations, including Cetus and Pisces. A very dark sky is required to see Aquarius.

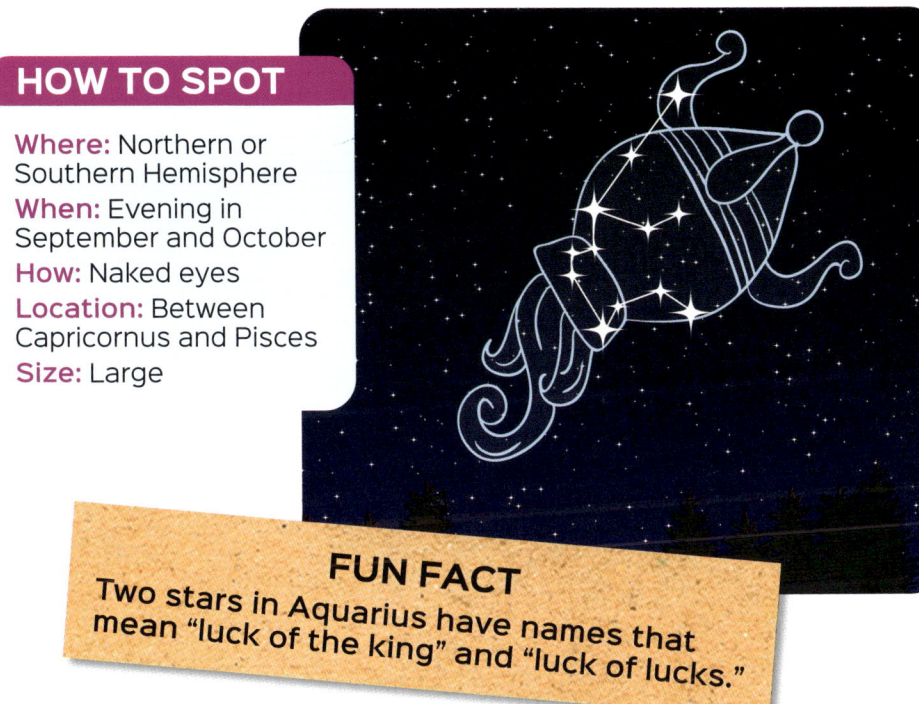

HOW TO SPOT

Where: Northern or Southern Hemisphere
When: Evening in September and October
How: Naked eyes
Location: Between Capricornus and Pisces
Size: Large

FUN FACT
Two stars in Aquarius have names that mean "luck of the king" and "luck of lucks."

THE ZODIAC SIGNS

Aquarius is one of 12 constellations that make up the zodiac. The others are Aries, Taurus, Gemini, Cancer, Leo, Virgo, Libra, Scorpius, Sagittarius, Capricornus, and Pisces. These constellations mark the path through the sky that the sun and the planets appear to follow. Horoscopes based on the zodiac are fun, but they are not at all scientific. The positions of distant stars can't influence people's lives.

CONSTELLATIONS

AQUILA *(THE EAGLE)*

The head, outstretched wings, and tail of Aquila form a plus sign. The name of Aquila's brightest star, Altair, means "bird" in Arabic. In the mythologies of China, Japan, and Korea, though, the star represents a herdsman who falls in love with a king's daughter. She is represented by the star Vega. The pair ends up banished to either side of the Milky Way, which represents a river. They can see each other only once every year. Tanabata, the Star Festival, is an annual holiday in Japan marking the day when the lovers are allowed to be together.

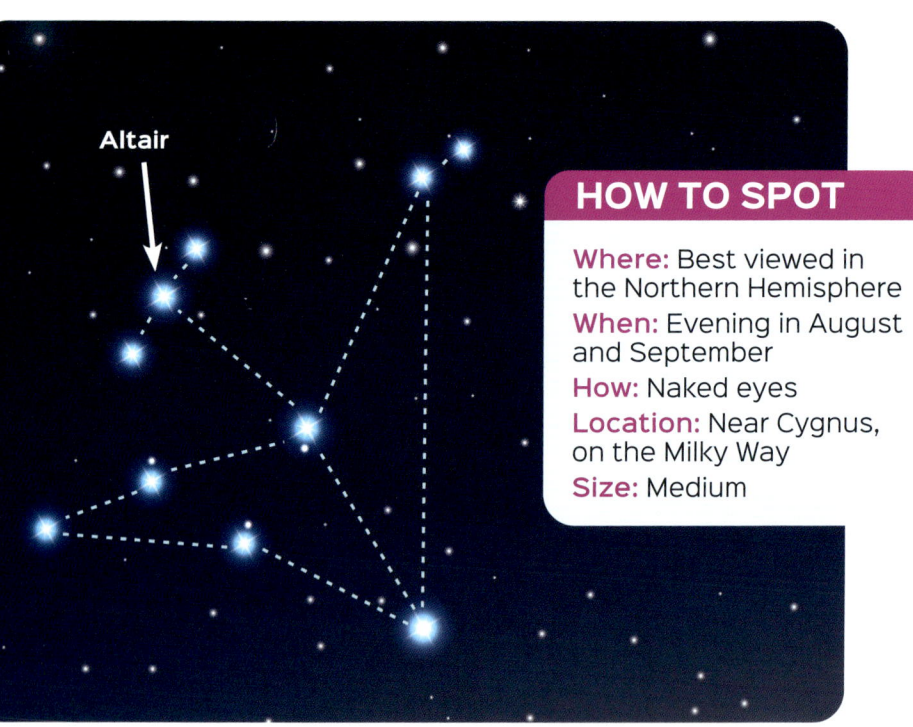

HOW TO SPOT

Where: Best viewed in the Northern Hemisphere
When: Evening in August and September
How: Naked eyes
Location: Near Cygnus, on the Milky Way
Size: Medium

FUN FACT
In Greek mythology, Aquila is the eagle that carried thunderbolts for Zeus.

ARIES *(THE RAM)*

In Greek mythology, Aries the ram had a fleece made of gold. A dragon guarded the fleece until the hero Jason stole it. Aries is the first of the 12 zodiac constellations, but it can be difficult to see. A dark sky is necessary to find it. The stars of Aries form a straight line that curves at one end.

HOW TO SPOT

Where: Northern or Southern Hemisphere
When: Evening in November and December
How: Naked eyes
Location: Between Pisces and Taurus
Size: Small

CONSTELLATIONS

BOÖTES *(THE HERDSMAN)*

Boötes (pronounced "boo-OH-tees") is visible from the Northern Hemisphere for most of the year. It is an easy constellation to spot because it contains Arcturus, one of the brightest stars. The handle of the Big Dipper points toward this star. The constellation is supposed to represent a person, but it looks more like a kite with Arcturus at its base. The famous ancient Greek story the *Odyssey* mentions Boötes.

HOW TO SPOT

Where: Northern Hemisphere
When: Best viewed in the evening in May and June
How: Naked eyes
Location: Near the Big Dipper
Size: Large

FUN FACT

An area of space near Boötes is almost empty of galaxies. Astronomers call it the Great Void.

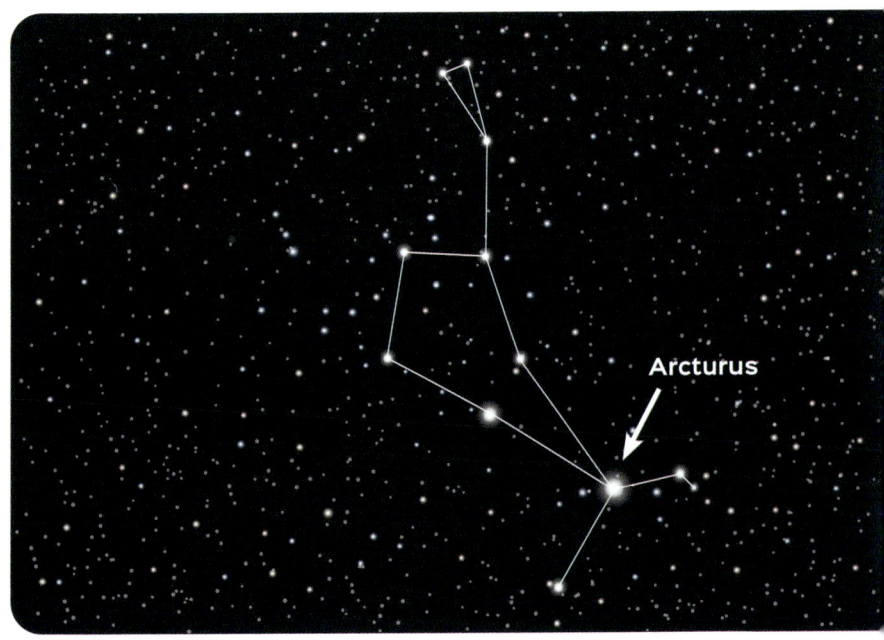

CANCER *(THE CRAB)*

Cancer is the dimmest of all the zodiac constellations, so a dark sky is necessary for viewing it. In the Northern Hemisphere, it looks like an upside-down letter Y. In the Southern Hemisphere, though, it looks right side up. In Greek mythology, the goddess Hera sent this crab to distract Heracles during a battle with the monster Hydra. According to one version of the story, the hero kicked the crab into the sky.

HOW TO SPOT

Where: Northern or Southern Hemisphere
When: Evening in March and April
How: Naked eyes
Location: Between Gemini and Leo
Size: Small

CONSTELLATIONS

CANIS MAJOR *(THE LARGER DOG)*

Canis Major contains the brightest star in the night sky, Sirius. The constellation is visible from the Northern Hemisphere during the winter just above the southern horizon. From the Southern Hemisphere, it climbs much higher in the sky. Canis Major and a nearby tiny constellation called Canis Minor (the Smaller Dog) seem to follow the constellation of Orion the Hunter across the sky. They represent his hunting dogs.

HOW TO SPOT

Where: Best viewed in the Southern Hemisphere
When: Evening in January and February
How: Naked eyes
Location: Following Orion
Size: Medium

FUN FACT
According to a Greek myth, Canis Major was the dog Laelaps, a hound so fast that no prey could escape it.

CAPRICORNUS *(THE SEA GOAT)*

The name Capricornus means "horned goat" in Latin, but this zodiac constellation is drawn as a mythical beast that is half goat and half fish. The ancient Sumerians and Babylonians called this constellation a goat-fish as far back as 2000 BCE. Capricornus is not very bright, but it forms a distinct triangular shape in a dark enough sky.

HOW TO SPOT

Where: Northern or Southern Hemisphere
When: Evening in August and September
How: Naked eyes
Location: Between Sagittarius and Aquarius
Size: Medium

CONSTELLATIONS

CASSIOPEIA *(THE QUEEN)*

Cassiopeia is one of the easiest constellations to identify. Its bright stars form a distinctive W shape that represents a seated woman. As it rotates around Polaris, the North Star, it sometimes looks more like an M instead. In Greek mythology, Queen Cassiopeia's boasting angers the gods, leading to her daughter Andromeda getting chained to a rock and Perseus rescuing her. The Sami people of Scandinavia saw this constellation as the antlers of a moose, and the Chukchi of Siberia saw it as a group of reindeer. Cassiopeia is visible all year in the Northern Hemisphere.

HOW TO SPOT

Where: Northern Hemisphere
When: Best viewed in the evening in October and November
How: Naked eyes
Location: Facing the North Star
Size: Medium

FUN FACT
In 1572, a bright new star appeared in Cassiopeia, fading after two years. It was actually a supernova, or an exploding star.

THE FIRST PEOPLE

Cassiopeia and the Big Dipper are located on opposite sides of the North Star. In Navajo tradition, these two constellations are Revolving Woman and Revolving Man. The North Star is their home fire. They represent the first people and lead all the other constellations.

CENTAURUS *(THE CENTAUR)*

Centaurus is a large and bright constellation that can be seen almost all year from the Southern Hemisphere. It is visible in parts of the Northern Hemisphere in May. In Greek mythology, Centaurus represents Chiron the centaur. He was a wise teacher who was half man and half horse. Two of the brightest stars in the sky, Alpha Centauri and Beta Centauri, form the front legs of the centaur.

HOW TO SPOT

Where: Southern Hemisphere
When: Best viewed in the evening in April and May
How: Naked eyes
Location: Wrapping around Crux
Size: Large

CONSTELLATIONS

CEPHEUS *(THE KING)*

In Greek mythology, Cepheus was Cassiopeia's husband and Andromeda's father. When the gods sent Cetus the sea monster toward Cepheus's kingdom, Cepheus asked an oracle what to do. The oracle told him he had to sacrifice his daughter to save everyone else. This constellation is very easy to spot. Its five bright stars resemble a house with a square bottom and a peaked roof. Cepheus is visible all year in the Northern Hemisphere but not from the Southern Hemisphere.

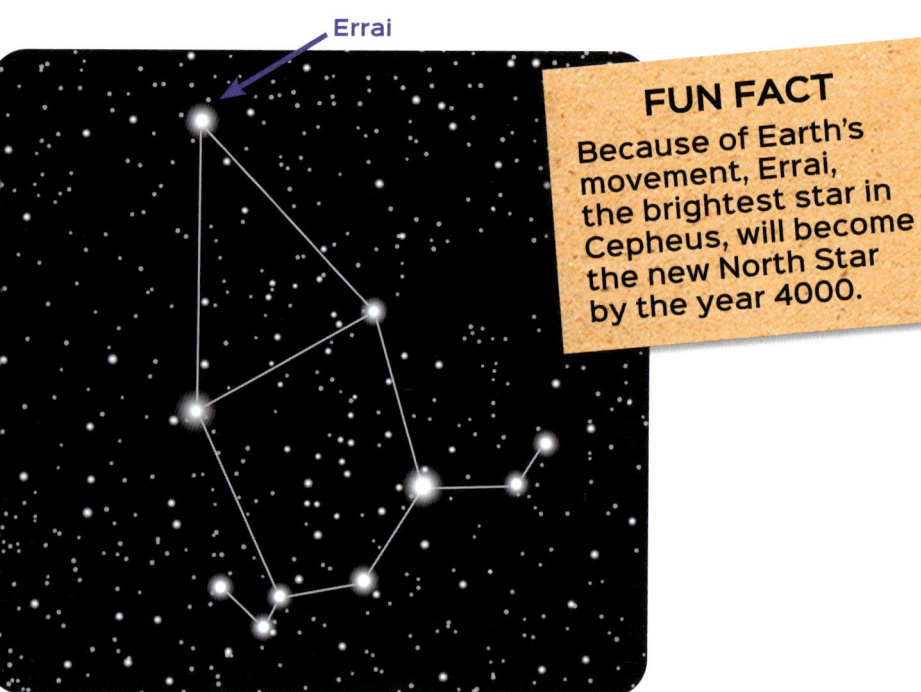

Errai

FUN FACT
Because of Earth's movement, Errai, the brightest star in Cepheus, will become the new North Star by the year 4000.

HOW TO SPOT

Where: Northern Hemisphere
When: Best viewed in the evening in September and October
How: Naked eyes
Location: Beside Cassiopeia
Size: Large

CETUS *(THE WHALE)*

Cetus is a very large but faint constellation located in the region of the sky known as the Sea. In Greek mythology, it represents the sea monster sent to devour Andromeda. Early Christians saw it as the whale that swallowed Jonah in a story from the Bible. The constellation looks like a small circle of stars connected to a larger oval-shaped group. The star that connects these two groups, Mira, was the first variable star ever discovered. Over 11 months, it gets quite bright, then fades until it is invisible to the naked eye.

HOW TO SPOT

Where: Northern or Southern Hemisphere
When: Best viewed in the evening in November
How: Naked eyes
Location: Near Pisces and Taurus
Size: Large

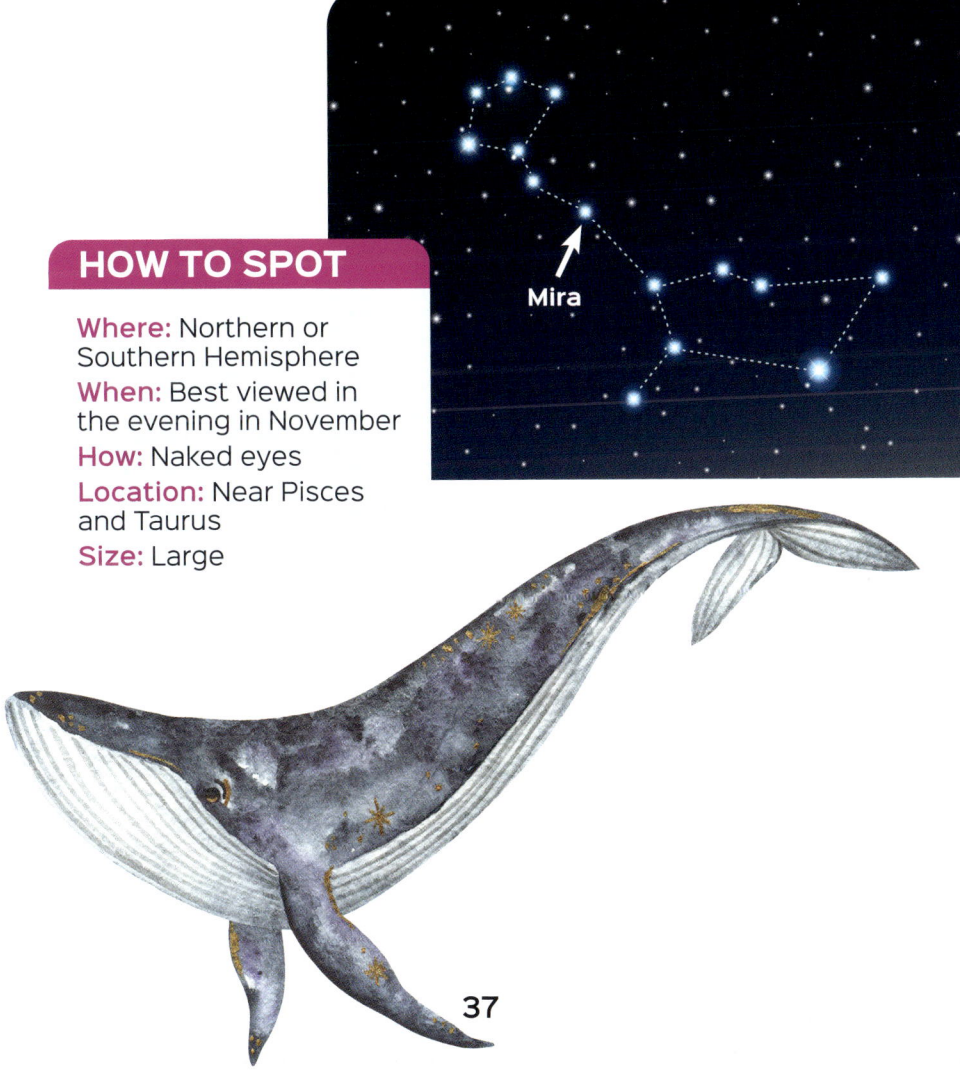

CONSTELLATIONS

CORONA BOREALIS
(THE NORTHERN CROWN)

Corona Borealis is a very small constellation, but it has a distinctive shape. It resembles a necklace or tiara. Fittingly, it represents a crown. In Greek mythology, this crown belonged to the princess Ariadne. She helped the hero Theseus escape from a labyrinth. In Celtic mythology, this constellation represents a castle called Caer Arianrhod where human souls go after they die. Some Aboriginal cultures in Australia have called this constellation a boomerang.

HOW TO SPOT

Where: Best viewed from the Northern Hemisphere
When: Evening in June and July
How: Naked eyes
Location: Between Boötes and Hercules
Size: Small

CRUX *(THE SOUTHERN CROSS)*

Crux may be small, but it is the most famous constellation in the Southern Hemisphere and is visible there almost any night of the year. Its four brightest stars form the shape of a cross or kite. Just as Ursa Major and the Big Dipper can be used to find north, this constellation helps a skilled navigator find south. Crux has featured in the mythology of many cultures. The Māori, who live in what is now New Zealand, see it as an anchor. In coastal Australia, it has been seen as a stingray, while inland it is an eagle's footprint.

HOW TO SPOT

Where: Southern Hemisphere
When: Best viewed in the evening in May
How: Naked eyes
Location: Surrounded on three sides by Centaurus
Size: Small

FUN FACT
The flag of Australia shows Crux.

CONSTELLATIONS

CYGNUS *(THE SWAN)*

The stars of Cygnus form the shape of a cross that represents a bird with outstretched wings. The bird seems to be flying down the Milky Way, so this constellation helps indicate the Milky Way's path through the sky. The brightest star in this constellation is called Deneb. It forms a shape called the Summer Triangle along with Altair and Vega. The central stars of Cygnus are also called the Northern Cross.

HOW TO SPOT

Where: Best viewed in the Northern Hemisphere
When: Evening in August and September
How: Naked eyes
Location: Aligned with the Milky Way, near Pegasus
Size: Large

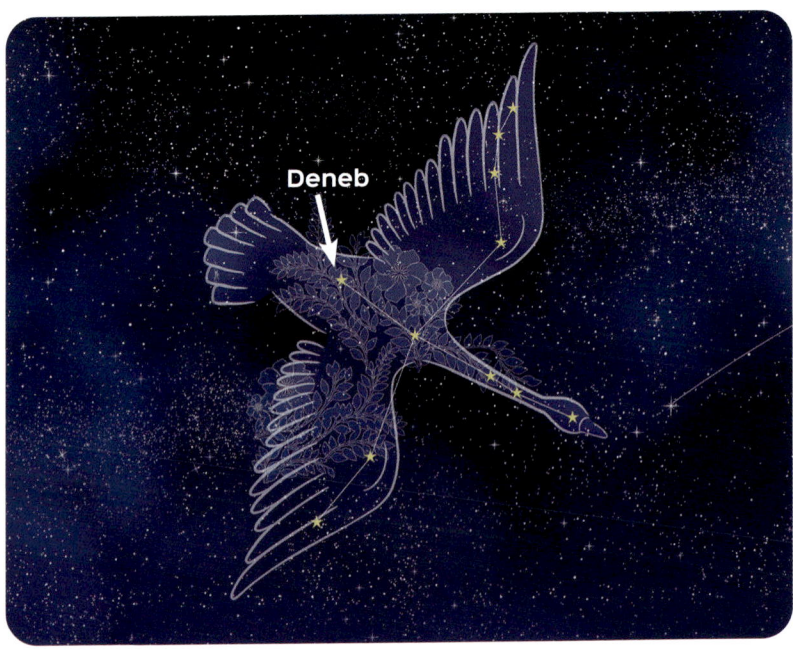

DRACO *(THE DRAGON)*

Draco is a large but not very bright constellation located right next to the North Star. Because of its position, Draco is visible all year from the Northern Hemisphere but never from the Southern Hemisphere. A small group of four stars forms the head of the constellation, which is a dragon. Its tail snakes around, ending between the Big and Little Dippers. Some early Christians identified Draco as the serpent from a story in the Bible.

HOW TO SPOT

Where: Northern Hemisphere

When: Best viewed in the evening in May and June

How: Naked eyes

Location: Beside Ursa Minor

Size: Large

FUN FACT
In Hindu tradition, Draco is an alligator. The ancient Egyptians saw it as a crocodile.

CONSTELLATIONS

ERIDANUS *(THE RIVER)*

Eridanus is a long but faint constellation that can be seen only in very dark skies. It forms the shape of a winding river. It represented the Euphrates to the Babylonians, the Nile to the ancient Egyptians, and the Ganges to the people of ancient India. The river begins near the hunter Orion's feet. In the Northern Hemisphere, it curves down and disappears behind the horizon. In Southern skies, it extends all the way to the bright star Achernar. This star's name means "the end of the river" in Arabic.

HOW TO SPOT

Where: Best viewed in the Southern Hemisphere
When: Evening in December and January
How: Naked eyes
Location: Beginning near Orion
Size: Large

GEMINI *(THE TWINS)*

Gemini looks like two stick figures holding hands. Their heads are two very bright stars located right next to each other named Castor and Pollux. In Greek mythology, Pollux was immortal, but his twin, Castor, was not. When Castor was killed, Pollux begged the gods to bring him back. Zeus agreed, but the twins had to spend half their time in the heavens. In China, these twin stars likely represented the concept of yin and yang. This is the idea that opposites, such as dark and light or male and female, must rely on each other.

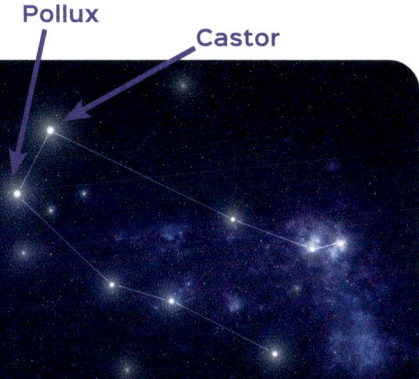

HOW TO SPOT

Where: Northern or Southern Hemisphere
When: Evening in February and March
How: Naked eyes
Location: Between Cancer and Taurus
Size: Medium

FUN FACT
Castor appears to be one star to the naked eye, but it is actually made up of three pairs of binary stars.

CONSTELLATIONS

HERCULES *(THE STRONGMAN)*

Hercules is the Roman name for Heracles, a hero from Greek mythology who is famous for his strength and cunning. During summertime in the Northern Hemisphere, Hercules is almost directly overhead. The stars of this constellation are not very bright, so a dark sky is best for viewing. A group of four stars forming a square-like shape called the Keystone make up his body. Bent legs and arms extend from the corners of this shape. One arm is sometimes shown holding a club.

HOW TO SPOT

Where: Best viewed in the Northern Hemisphere
When: Evening in July and August
How: Naked eyes
Location: Between the stars Arcturus and Vega
Size: Large

DEFEATING THE DRAGON

In the story of the 12 labors of Hercules, the hero completes seemingly impossible tasks. One task is to pick golden apples guarded by a hundred-headed dragon. Hercules kills the dragon, Draco. In the night sky, the hero seems to be standing on Draco's head.

HYDRA *(THE SEA SERPENT)*

Hydra is the largest constellation in the night sky, but it is not very bright. Representing a long, winding sea serpent, it is a zigzagging line of stars that extends the length of four zodiac constellations. At one end, a small, kite-shaped group of stars forms the monster's head. In Greek mythology, Heracles had to fight Hydra as one of his 12 tasks. Every time he destroyed one head, two more grew in its place.

HOW TO SPOT

Where: Best viewed in the Southern Hemisphere

When: Evening in March and April

How: Naked eyes

Location: Extending from Libra to Cancer

Size: Very Large

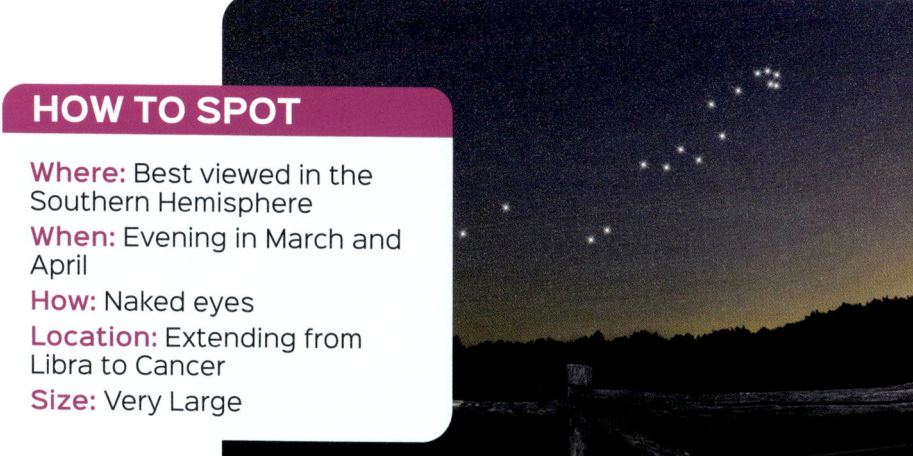

CONSTELLATIONS

LEO *(THE LION)*

Leo is a zodiac constellation that is fairly easy to find. The brightest stars form the shape of a backward question mark, with the bright, blue-white star Regulus at the bottom. This group of stars is also called the Sickle. It represents the head and chest of a lion. More stars extend out behind this shape to form the lion's body. In Greek mythology, Leo was a lion with a hide that no weapon could pierce. Heracles defeated it and placed it in the sky.

FUN FACT
The shape of the Sphinx in Egypt may have been inspired by the constellation Leo.

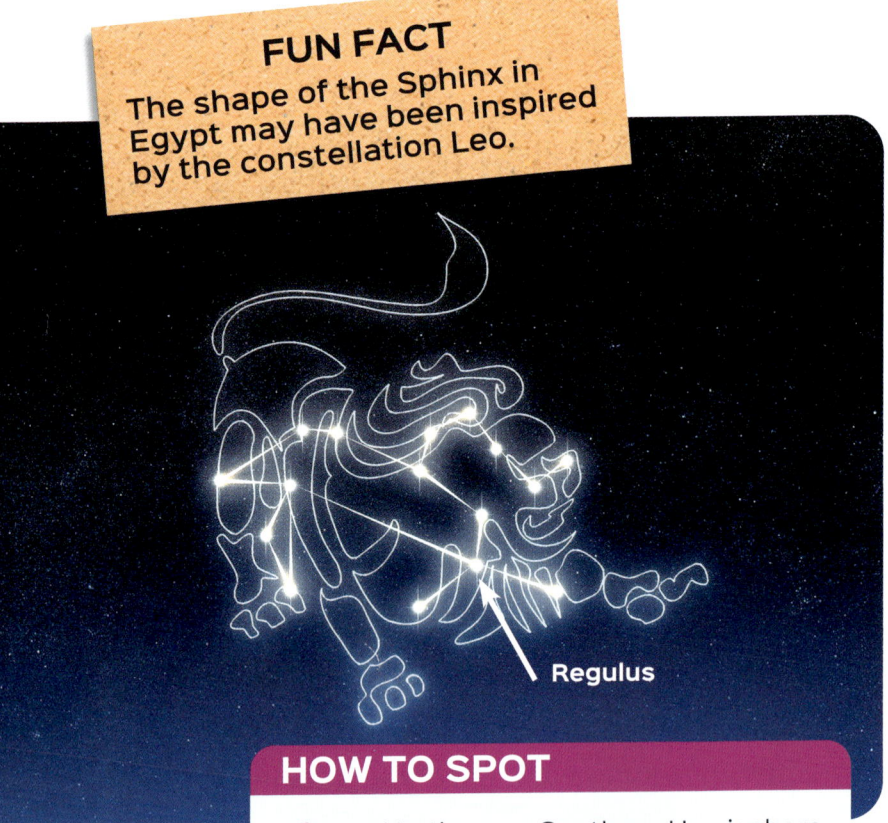

HOW TO SPOT

Where: Northern or Southern Hemisphere
When: Evening in March and April
How: Naked eyes
Location: Between Virgo and Cancer
Size: Large

LIBRA *(THE SCALES)*

Libra is the only zodiac constellation that doesn't represent a person or animal. Instead, it is an old-fashioned scale that would have been used to weigh goods. It looks like a triangle with two lines extending down. The ancient Greeks combined this constellation with Scorpius, turning it into the scorpion's claws. The Romans named it a scale. They may have done so because the sun passed through Libra during the autumn equinox, when day and night have equal lengths.

HOW TO SPOT

Where: Northern or Southern Hemisphere
When: Evening in June and July
How: Naked eyes
Location: Between Virgo and Scorpius
Size: Medium

CONSTELLATIONS

LYRA *(THE LYRE)*

Lyra is a small but distinct constellation that is visible for most of the year in the Northern Hemisphere. It represents an ancient Greek stringed instrument called a lyre. It looks like a tilted rectangle stuck to a triangle. One of the saddest stories in Greek mythology involves this constellation. The musician Orpheus's wife dies, so he plays this lyre for the god of death. Orpheus is allowed to have his wife back if he leads her to the land of the living without looking back. At the last minute, the musician turns around and loses his wife forever.

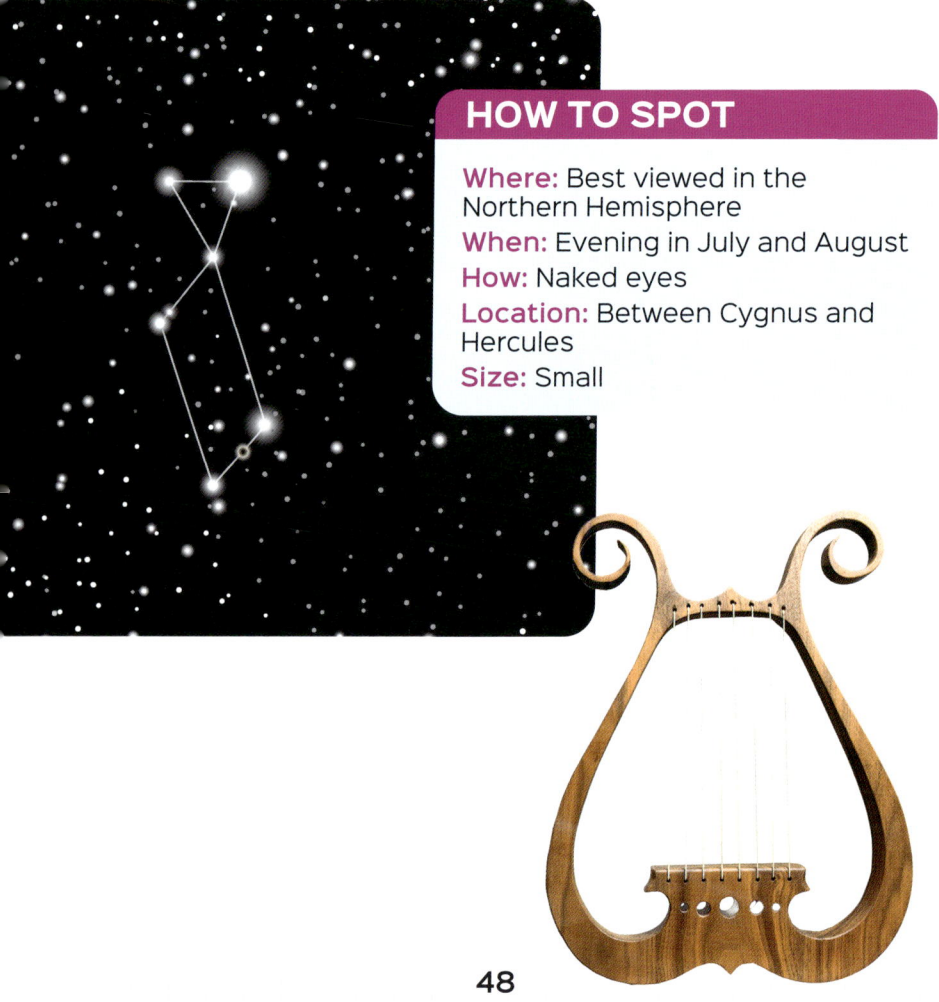

HOW TO SPOT

Where: Best viewed in the Northern Hemisphere
When: Evening in July and August
How: Naked eyes
Location: Between Cygnus and Hercules
Size: Small

OPHIUCHUS AND SERPENS
(THE SERPENT BEARER AND THE SERPENT)

Ophiuchus (pronounced "off-ee-YOO-kiss") and Serpens rotate along the same path as the sun and planets with the 12 zodiac constellations. But Ophiuchus and Serpens are not part of the zodiac constellations. The ancient Babylonians thought 13 was an unlucky number, so they divided the zodiac into just 12 signs to match the 12 months of the year. This faint pair of constellations represents a man carrying a snake. Serpens the snake is a symbol of healing.

FUN FACT
If Ophiuchus were part of the zodiac, it would be the sign for people born between November 29 and December 17.

HOW TO SPOT

Where: Northern or Southern Hemisphere
When: Evening in June and July
How: Naked eyes
Location: Between Sagittarius and Scorpius
Size: Large

CONSTELLATIONS

ORION *(THE HUNTER)*

Orion is perhaps the most famous and easily recognized constellation. It is visible all over the world, even in places with a lot of light pollution. The easiest part to notice is Orion's belt, a chain of three very bright stars. The brightest star in the constellation, Betelgeuse, marks the hunter's shoulder. Many cultures all around the world have identified this constellation as a heroic figure. In some African cultures, the belt stars represent animals, including zebras, pigs, or tortoises.

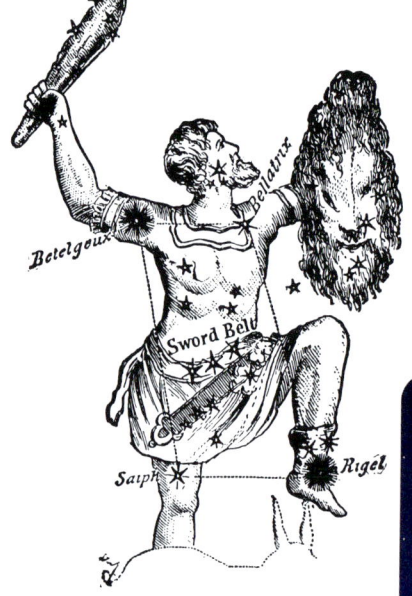

HOW TO SPOT

Where: Northern or Southern Hemisphere
When: Evening in January and February
How: Naked eyes
Location: Near Canis Major
Size: Medium

Betelgeuse

PEGASUS *(THE WINGED HORSE)*

In Greek mythology, Pegasus was a flying horse that played a part in several stories. In one myth, Perseus rode Pegasus to rescue Andromeda. All of these constellations are located together in the sky. The stars of Pegasus are not very bright. However, four of the stars form the shape of a square, so this constellation is easy to recognize in a dark sky. Sky watchers use the square of Pegasus to help find other interesting sights.

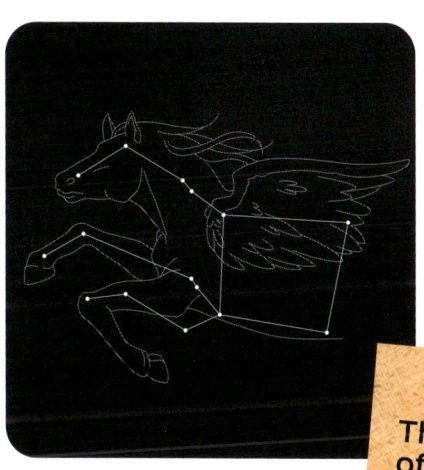

HOW TO SPOT

Where: Northern or Southern Hemisphere
When: Evening in September and October
How: Naked eyes
Location: Near Andromeda and Cassiopeia
Size: Large

FUN FACT
The Ojibwa people of North America have called this constellation a moose.

THE SEARCH FOR EXOPLANETS

Planets orbiting other stars are called exoplanets. More than 4,000 have been discovered. Astronomers have found many of them by looking for patterns in the way stars shine. Stars dim slightly when planets pass in front of them. In other cases, astronomers find exoplanets by noticing how the planets' gravity affects stars' motions. In 1995, the first exoplanet orbiting a sun-like star was detected in Pegasus. The scientists who found it earned the Nobel Prize in physics in 2019.

CONSTELLATIONS

PERSEUS *(THE HERO)*

Perseus is a famous hero from Greek mythology. His constellation lies in the Milky Way. It is in the same section of sky as Cassiopeia, Pegasus, and Andromeda, whom Perseus rescued from Cetus the sea monster. Perseus is a fairly bright constellation that is visible almost all year in the Northern Hemisphere. It represents the hero holding the head of the monster Medusa with his sword raised. The star Algol, also called the demon star, represents the eye of Medusa. It gets dimmer every three days, as if it is winking.

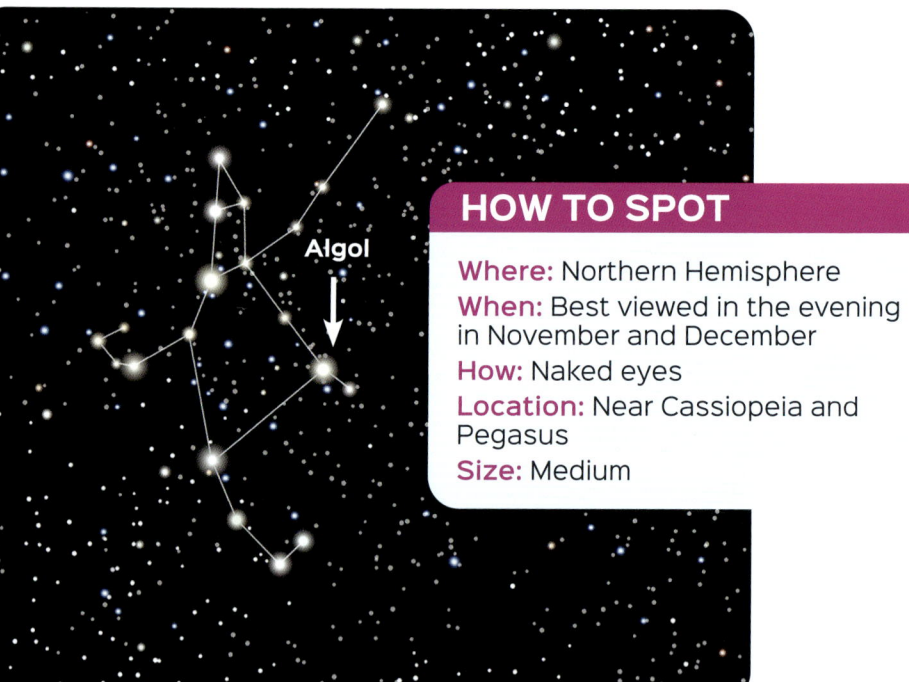

HOW TO SPOT

Where: Northern Hemisphere
When: Best viewed in the evening in November and December
How: Naked eyes
Location: Near Cassiopeia and Pegasus
Size: Medium

PERSEUS AND MEDUSA

In Greek mythology, Medusa was a monster with a woman's body and hair made of snakes. Anyone who saw her turned to stone. Perseus managed to cut off her head by looking only at her reflection in his mirror-like shield. Pegasus was born from Medusa's blood.

PISCES *(THE FISH)*

Pisces represents two fish tied together with string. It resembles a large V shape. A small circle of stars at one end of the V's arms is called the Circlet. The V shape opens toward the square of Pegasus. This zodiac constellation is dim, so a dark sky is required to see it. In Greek and Roman mythology, the two fish are the goddess of love and her son. They transformed into fish and tied themselves together to escape a sea monster.

HOW TO SPOT

Where: Northern or Southern Hemisphere
When: Evening in October and November
How: Naked eyes
Location: Between Aries and Aquarius
Size: Large

CONSTELLATIONS

SAGITTARIUS *(THE ARCHER)*

Sagittarius is one of the 12 zodiac constellations. It is depicted as a centaur, or a half-man, half-horse creature, holding a bow and arrow. The easiest part of the constellation to see forms a shape that closely resembles a teapot. Sagittarius is bright and visible for most of the year in the Southern Hemisphere. In the Northern Hemisphere, it peeks above the horizon during July and August.

HOW TO SPOT

Where: Best viewed from the Southern Hemisphere

When: Evening in July and August in the Northern Hemisphere

How: Naked eyes

Location: Between Capricornus and Scorpius

Size: Large

FUN FACT
Sagittarius marks the center of the Milky Way galaxy.

SCORPIUS *(THE SCORPION)*

Scorpius is a zodiac constellation that is best viewed from the Southern Hemisphere. In northern skies, it can be seen only near the horizon. Scorpius is one of the easiest constellations to find because its bright stars form the shape of a capital letter J. The bright-orange star Antares marks the heart of the scorpion. In Greek mythology, the hunter Orion died after stepping on this scorpion. Orion and Scorpius never appear together in the sky.

HOW TO SPOT

Where: Best viewed from the Southern Hemisphere
When: Evening in July and August
How: Naked eyes
Location: Between Sagittarius and Libra
Size: Medium

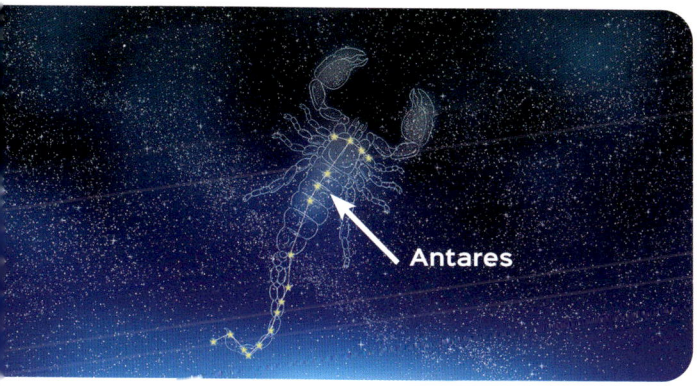

THE FOUR SYMBOLS

Ancient Chinese astronomers divided the sky into four very large constellations. A green dragon in the east included Scorpius, Libra, and Sagittarius. There was also a red bird in the south, a white tiger in the west, and a black tortoise in the north.

CONSTELLATIONS

TAURUS *(THE BULL)*

Of the 12 zodiac constellations, Taurus is probably the easiest to find. It is visible from all over the world, and its brightest stars outshine light pollution. Orion's belt points toward the brightest star in Taurus, Aldebaran. To the ancient Egyptians, Taurus represented the Apis bull. This was a sacred animal believed to contain the spirit of the god Osiris. The famous star cluster known as the Pleiades forms the bull's shoulder.

HOW TO SPOT

Where: Northern or Southern Hemisphere
When: Evening in January and February
How: Naked eyes
Location: Next to Orion
Size: Large

URSA MAJOR *(THE GREAT BEAR)*

In Greek mythology, the gods transformed a beautiful nymph named Callisto into a bear. The brightest stars of Ursa Major form the Big Dipper, one of the most famous groups of stars in the world. From the Northern Hemisphere, Ursa Major and the Big Dipper stay visible year-round.

HOW TO SPOT

Where: Northern Hemisphere
When: Best viewed in the evening in March and April
How: Naked eyes
Location: Tail and back are formed in part by the Big Dipper
Size: Large

FUN FACT
Ancient Egyptians called this constellation the Hippopotamus.

FINDING NORTH

Harriet Tubman and other people who had been enslaved in the southern United States used the stars to find their way north to freedom. The folk song "Follow the Drinking Gourd" tells of these journeys. The Drinking Gourd is another name for the Big Dipper. The two stars that make up the front side of the Big Dipper form a line that points to the North Star, which always hangs over the North Pole.

CONSTELLATIONS

URSA MINOR *(THE LITTLE BEAR)*

Ursa Minor is made up in part by the Little Dipper. This collection of stars matches the shape of the larger Big Dipper. The Little Dipper looks as if it is pouring into the larger one. Polaris, the North Star, is at the end of the Little Dipper's handle. The stars of this constellation aren't very bright, so a dark sky offers the best chance to see them.

HOW TO SPOT

Where: Northern Hemisphere
When: All year
How: Naked eyes
Location: Near Ursa Major
Size: Small

Polaris

FUN FACT
The Ojibwa people of North America saw Ursa Minor as a loon.

VIRGO *(THE VIRGIN)*

Virgo is the largest zodiac constellation and the only one that represents a woman. It isn't very bright. In an area with light pollution, only its brightest star, Spica, may be visible. Spica appears blueish white in color. Virgo is usually shown holding wheat and has been associated with many different goddesses. Virgo is also the location of the most distant object visible to a small telescope. It is a bright light source called a quasar that is 3 billion light-years away.

HOW TO SPOT

Where: Northern or Southern Hemisphere
When: Evening in May and June
How: Naked eyes
Location: Between Libra and Leo
Size: Large

THE RETURN OF SPRING

Virgo returns to the sky in spring. This matches the story of Persephone. She was a Greek goddess who had to stay in the underworld for half of the year. During this time, it was winter. When she returned, her mother, the goddess Demeter, let the world grow and bloom again.

STARS

ALDEBARAN

Aldebaran is a red giant, a type of star that is nearing the end of its life cycle. These stars are huge, up to hundreds of times larger than the sun. However, they are not as hot. Aldebaran's surface burns at approximately 6,700 degrees Fahrenheit (3,704°C), while the sun's surface is 10,000 degrees Fahrenheit (5,538°C). The name Aldebaran means "the follower" in Arabic. This star appears to follow the Pleiades star cluster, which was the most important night sky object in ancient Arabia.

HOW TO SPOT

Where: Northern or Southern Hemisphere
When: Evening in January and February
How: Naked eyes
Location: Taurus
Distance: 67 light-years from Earth
Magnitude: +0.9
Color: Red-orange

A STAR'S DEATH

When a star runs out of fuel, it expands into a large red giant that slowly drifts apart. The leftover core is called a white dwarf. A very large star becomes a red supergiant, eventually exploding in a massive supernova. This may leave behind a black hole.

ALPHA CENTAURI

Alpha Centauri has two companion stars. Beta Centauri appears nearby in the sky. These two stars form the front hooves of the constellation Centaurus. The third star, Proxima Centauri, is visible only through a telescope. This star system is the sun's nearest neighbor. Alpha Centauri is not visible north of Orlando, Florida.

HOW TO SPOT

Where: Southern Hemisphere
When: Best viewed in the evening in April and May
How: Naked eyes
Location: Centaurus
Distance: 4.4 light-years from Earth
Magnitude: 0.0
Color: Yellow

An artist's vision of the planet Proxima b

PLANETS AT THE ALPHA CENTAURI SYSTEM

Astronomers have found two planets orbiting Proxima Centauri. The planet Proxima b is around the same size as Earth. It is close enough to the star that water could remain liquid on the surface. It may be possible for life to exist there. Studying this planet won't be easy, though. It would take today's spacecraft 80,000 years to get there.

STARS

ANTARES

Antares is a red supergiant located in the constellation Scorpius. The Romans called it the heart of the scorpion. Antares is so huge that if it were the width of a basketball court, the sun would be the width of a penny. Antares is visible year-round in the Southern Hemisphere. Every few years, Mars passes near this star. The planet and star are both red, so people regularly confuse the two. This likely happened in ancient times as well; the name Antares means "Not Mars" or "Rival of Mars" in Greek.

In 2017, scientists with the European Southern Observatory created an image of Antares, the most detailed image ever of a star other than the sun.

HOW TO SPOT

Where: Best viewed from the Southern Hemisphere
When: Evening in July and August
How: Naked eyes
Location: Scorpius
Distance: 554 light-years from Earth
Magnitude: +1.1
Color: Red

ARCTURUS

Arcturus is the fourth-brightest star in the entire night sky. It is the brightest one visible in the Northern Hemisphere for most of the year. Extending the curve, or arc, of the handle of the Big Dipper leads to this star. A handy way to remember this is the phrase "arc to Arcturus." The name Arcturus means "guardian of the bear." That's because the star seems to follow the Big Dipper, which is part of Ursa Major (the Great Bear), around the sky. This star is a red giant.

FUN FACT
Most stars rotate through the Milky Way in a flat, spiral shape. Arcturus travels up and down around the galaxy with a small group of other stars.

HOW TO SPOT

Where: Northern Hemisphere
When: Best viewed in the evening in May and June
How: Naked eyes
Location: Boötes
Distance: 36 light-years from Earth
Magnitude: 0.0
Color: Orange-red

STARS
BETELGEUSE

One the largest stars visible to the naked eye, Betelgeuse is a red supergiant, a massive star that is nearing the end of its life. At some point in the next 100,000 years, Betelgeuse will explode in a supernova. Some people thought this was starting to happen in 2019 because the star dimmed unexpectedly. Astronomers figured out that Betelgeuse had actually just belched out a cloud of gas that blocked some of the star's light. This star marks one shoulder of the constellation Orion. In some myths, the red star represents a wound on the hero.

FUN FACT
The name Betelgeuse comes from Arabic. One possible translation is "armpit of the giant."

HOW TO SPOT

Where: Northern or Southern Hemisphere
When: Evening in January and February
How: Naked eyes
Location: Orion
Distance: 530 light-years from Earth
Magnitude: Up to 0.0
Color: Red

CANOPUS

Canopus is the second-brightest star in the night sky, but in many parts of the Northern Hemisphere it is never visible. In the Southern Hemisphere, this supergiant star rises high in the sky. It is part of the southern constellation Carina, which represents the keel of a ship. In many parts of southern Africa, Canopus is called Naka, meaning "the Horn Star." Traditionally, the first person to see the star rise would play a horn and might earn a cow as a reward.

HOW TO SPOT

Where: Southern Hemisphere
When: Best viewed in the evening in February
How: Naked eyes
Location: Carina
Distance: 309 light-years from Earth
Magnitude: -0.7
Color: Yellow-white

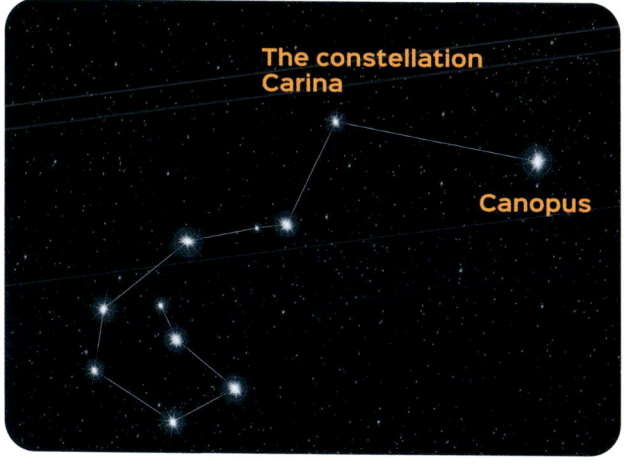

The constellation Carina

Canopus

STARS

CAPELLA

Capella is also called the Goat Star. Today it is part of the constellation Auriga, which represents a person driving a chariot. But in some ancient stories, the constellation was a person herding goats. A faint group of three stars near Capella represented baby goats. Capella itself is actually a four-star system. The two brightest stars are almost the same size and color. It takes a powerful telescope at an observatory to see them separately. The other two stars are small red dwarfs.

HOW TO SPOT

Where: Best viewed in the Northern Hemisphere
When: Evening in December and January
How: Naked eyes
Location: Auriga
Distance: 43 light-years from Earth
Magnitude: +0.1
Color: Yellow

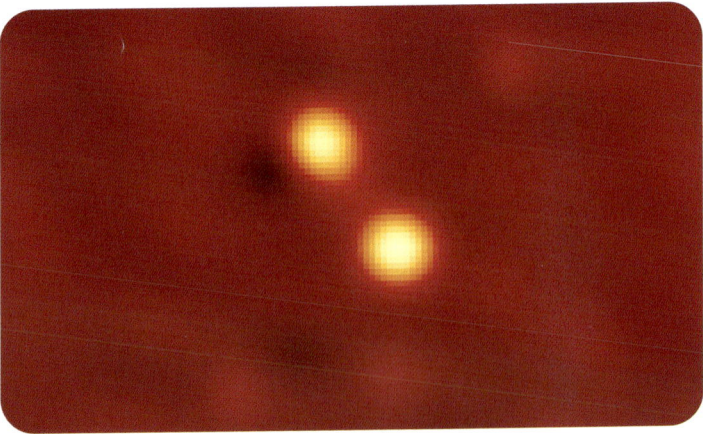

Powerful telescopes can reveal the two distinct bright stars in Capella.

CASTOR AND POLLUX

The twin stars of the constellation Gemini, Castor and Pollux, appear right next to each other in the sky. In fact, several light-years separate these stars. And they certainly aren't identical twins. Castor is actually a star system containing six separate stars. Pollux is a larger red giant that shines more brightly than Castor with a distinctive yellow-orange or golden color.

HOW TO SPOT

Where: Northern or Southern Hemisphere

When: Evening in February to March

How: Naked eyes

Location: Gemini

Distance: 51 light-years (Castor) and 33 light-years (Pollux) from Earth

Magnitude: +1.6 (Castor) and +1.2 (Pollux)

Color: Blue-white (Castor) and yellow-orange (Pollux)

FUN FACT
An exoplanet named Thestias orbits Pollux. It is at least twice the size of Jupiter.

STARS
DENEB

Deneb is one of the most distant stars that is visible to the naked eye. Astronomers estimate that it is more than 2,000 light-years away. The farther away a light source is, the dimmer it appears. Yet Deneb is one of the brighter stars in the sky. It shines up to 200,000 times brighter than the sun. Deneb and the stars Altair and Vega form a shape called the Summer Triangle because in northern skies they rise very high in the summer. In Chinese, Japanese, and Korean mythologies, Altair and Vega represent a pair of lovers who are allowed to meet only once a year. Deneb represents a bridge between them.

Deneb

FUN FACT
If Deneb took the sun's place in our solar system, Earth would have to be located much farther away from it to get the same amount of light it does currently. Earth would need to be nine times farther away from the sun than Pluto is now.

HOW TO SPOT

Where: Best viewed in the Northern Hemisphere
When: Evening in August and September
How: Naked eyes
Location: Cygnus
Distance: More than 2,000 light-years from Earth
Magnitude: +1.3
Color: Blue-white

ETA CARINAE

Eta Carinae is a dying star system containing two huge stars that orbit each other closely. Back in 1838, these stars seemed to explode in an event called the Great Eruption. For more than a decade, Eta Carinae was the second-brightest star in the entire sky. It then faded and is now barely visible to the naked eye. Twin clouds of dust and gas from that eruption form a peanut shape around the star system.

HOW TO SPOT

Where: Southern Hemisphere
When: Best viewed in the evening in February
How: Naked eyes
Location: Carina
Distance: 7,500 light-years from Earth
Magnitude: Varies; currently +4.5
Color: Multicolored

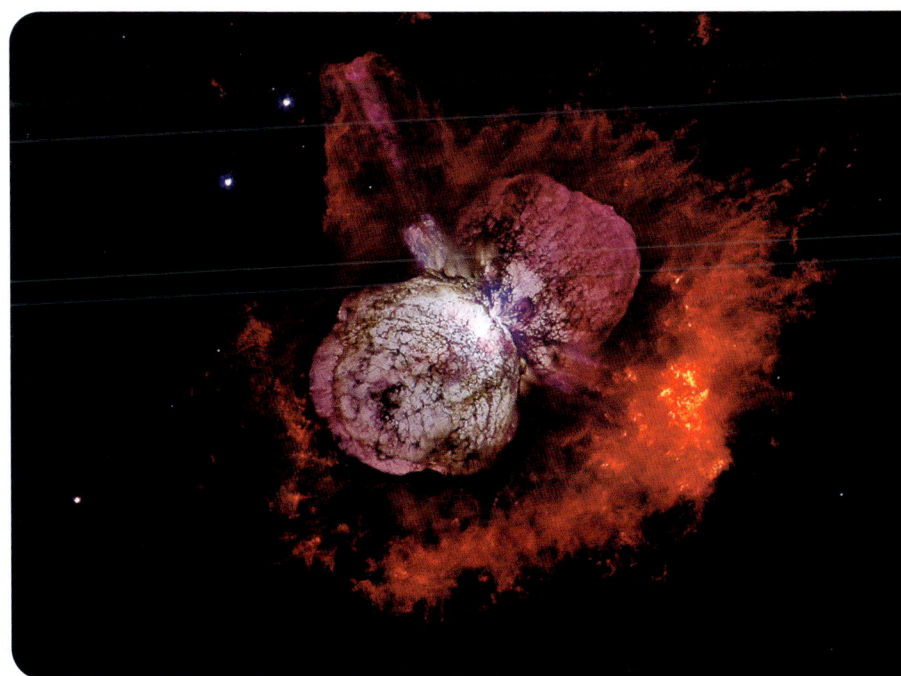

STARS

FOMALHAUT

Fomalhaut comes from a phrase meaning "mouth of the fish" in Arabic. This star is the brightest one in the constellation Piscis Austrinus, also known as the Southern Fish. Fomalhaut is one of the sun's nearest neighbors. It is just 100 to 300 million years old, which is young for a star. Most stars shine for billions of years. Fomalhaut is nicknamed "the lonely one" since it shines from a fairly dark and empty part of the sky. The western side of the Great Square of Pegasus points toward this star.

HOW TO SPOT

Where: Best viewed in the Southern Hemisphere
When: Evening in September and October
How: Naked eyes
Location: Piscis Austrinus
Distance: 25 light-years from Earth
Magnitude: +1.2
Color: Blue-white

THE ROYAL STARS

The ancient Persians recognized four "royal stars" as guardians of the sky and markers of the seasons. Regulus, the leader of the stars, indicated spring. Antares brought summer. Fomalhaut was the autumn star, and Aldebaran marked winter.

MIZAR AND ALCOR

Mizar is located in the middle of the Big Dipper's handle. In a very dark sky or through binoculars, a second, fainter star is visible just beside Mizar. This is Alcor. This pair was the first binary star system ever discovered. Astronomers later realized that these twins are actually sextuplets. Mizar is a set of four stars, and Alcor is a set of two.

HOW TO SPOT

Where: Northern Hemisphere
When: Best viewed in the evening in March and April
How: Naked eyes
Location: Ursa Major
Distance: 80 light-years from Earth
Magnitude: +2.0 (Mizar) and +4.0 (Alcor)
Color: White to blue-white

FUN FACT
In ancient Arabia, Mizar and Alcor were called the horse and rider.

STARS

POLARIS *(THE NORTH STAR)*

Polaris may be the most famous star in the northern sky, even though it is not very bright. Commonly known as the North Star, it seems to remain in place above Earth's North Pole while all the other stars spin around it. This means it is always visible from the Northern Hemisphere, but it can never be seen from any location south of the equator. For centuries, navigators have used it to locate north and to determine latitude, or how close someone is to the equator. In Mongolian mythology, Polaris holds the world together.

HOW TO SPOT

Where: Northern Hemisphere
When: All year
How: Naked eyes
Location: The end of the Little Dipper's handle
Distance: 433 light-years from Earth
Magnitude: +2.0
Color: Yellow-white

FUN FACT
The indigo bunting and some other bird species migrate at night, using the rotation of stars around Polaris to find their way.

THE HIGHEST PEAK

In a story from the Paiute of North America, Polaris is the mountain sheep Na-gah. He climbed the highest mountain peak and had no way back down. His sorrowful father transformed him into a star that lights the way for anyone who is lost.

PROCYON

Procyon is part of the constellation Canis Minor, or Smaller Dog. Along with Betelgeuse in Orion and Sirius in Canis Major, Procyon forms a shape called the Winter Triangle. Procyon is one of the sun's closest neighbors. It is a binary system of two stars, one of which is a white dwarf. In ancient Arabian mythology, Procyon and Sirius represented two sisters and Canopus was their brother. After a tragic event, Canopus and Sirius fled across the Milky Way. Procyon was left behind.

HOW TO SPOT

Where: Northern or Southern Hemisphere
When: Evening in January and February
How: Naked eyes
Location: Canis Minor
Distance: 12 light-years from Earth
Magnitude: +0.3
Color: Yellow

STARS

REGULUS

Regulus has long been associated with royalty. Its name is Latin for "little king." Regulus is also nicknamed "heart of the lion" because of its position in the zodiac constellation Leo. A lion is often called the king of the beasts. Regulus is located near the path that the sun and planets take through the sky. This means that occasionally a planet passes in front of Regulus, hiding the star from view. Venus will eclipse Regulus in 2044.

HOW TO SPOT

Where: Northern or Southern Hemisphere
When: Evening in March and April
How: Naked eyes
Location: Leo
Distance: 79 light-years from Earth
Magnitude: +1.4
Color: Blue-white

FUN FACT
Regulus spins so quickly that it has a distinct oval shape. If it spun a little faster, it would fly apart.

Regulus

RIGEL

Rigel is an extremely hot star, more than twice as hot as the sun. It is a supergiant star that is 75 times the width of the sun. Rigel is part of a multistar system. Rigel A is orbited by a pair of smaller stars called Rigel B. This star system marks one foot of the constellation Orion. In one Inuit story, Orion's belt is a trio of hunters following a polar bear. Rigel is a fourth hunter who dropped his glove and had to stop to get it.

HOW TO SPOT

Where: Northern or Southern Hemisphere
When: Evening in January and February
How: Naked eyes
Location: Orion
Distance: 863 light-years from Earth
Magnitude: +0.1
Color: Blue-white

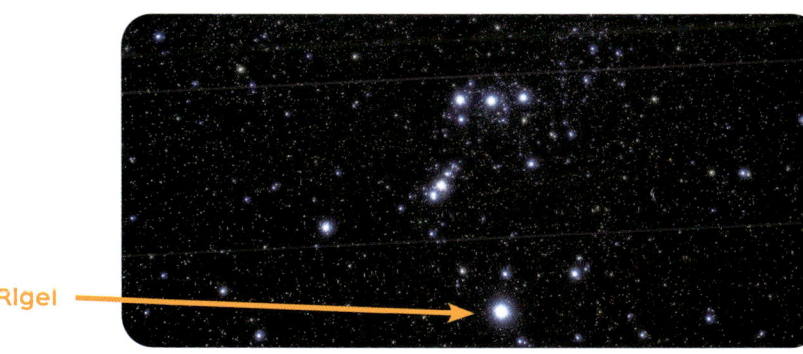

Rigel

STAR COLORS

A star's color reveals the temperature of its outer layer. The hottest stars appear blue-white, average ones like the sun appear yellow, and the coolest stars seem orange or red. The constellation Orion contains the red star Betelgeuse and the blue-white star Rigel. Star colors are easiest to see using binoculars or telescopes.

STARS

SIRIUS

Sirius is the brightest star in the entire night sky. It is larger than the sun and puts out much more light. However, the main reason it outshines all other stars is that it is located fairly near Earth. Sirius is called the Dog Star because it is part of Canis Major, which represents a dog. Though it is the brightest star, Sirius is not the brightest object in the night sky. The moon and planets can all outshine it because they are so much closer to Earth. Sirius can be found by following the line formed by the three stars in Orion's belt toward the southeast.

HOW TO SPOT

Where: Best viewed in the Southern Hemisphere
When: Evening in January and February
How: Naked eyes
Location: Canis Major
Distance: 8.6 light-years from Earth
Magnitude: -1.5
Color: Blue-white

Sirius B can be seen immediately below and to the right of Sirius A.

COMPANION STARS

Sirius is officially known as Sirius A. It is part of a binary star system, meaning two stars that orbit each other. Astronomers discovered Sirius B in 1862. Nicknamed "the Pup," Sirius B is smaller than Earth. It is a white dwarf, a type of star that has burned through all its fuel.

VEGA

Vega is a bright star more than twice the size of the sun. It is part of the summer triangle with Altair and Deneb. Vega's constellation is Lyra, a very small but bright constellation. Vega is most likely a young star. Astronomers believe that a cloud of dust around the star could mean that planets are forming there. In Chinese, Japanese, and Korean mythologies, Vega represents a king's daughter who is separated from her lover, the star Altair. They are separated by a river represented by the Milky Way.

FUN FACT
Vega was the North Star in 12,000 BCE. It will be in this position in the sky again by 13,700 CE.

HOW TO SPOT

Where: Best viewed in the Northern Hemisphere
When: Evening in July and August
How: Naked eyes
Location: Lyra
Distance: 25 light-years from Earth
Magnitude: 0.0
Color: Blue-white

STAR CLUSTERS

ALPHA PERSEI MOVING GROUP

The brightest star in the constellation Perseus is called Mirfak, Arabic for "elbow." It shines brightly even in a night sky with light pollution. But it's not alone. In a very dark sky, it's possible to see dozens of other stars surrounding it. Binoculars help improve the view. These stars form the Alpha Persei Moving Group. As the name implies, the stars are not staying in place. They have been moving through space for the past 30 to 50 million years, since they formed. These stars are also called the Attendants of Mirfak.

FUN FACT
In native Hawaiian tradition, Mirfak marked the separation point between Earth and sky during the creation of the Milky Way.

HOW TO SPOT

Where: Northern Hemisphere
When: Best viewed in the evening in November and December
How: Naked eyes or binoculars
Location: Perseus
Distance: 506 light-years from Earth
Magnitude: +1.8 (Mirfak)

Mirfak

BEEHIVE CLUSTER

The Beehive Cluster is a group of about 1,000 stars sitting in the middle of the constellation Cancer. It fills a space in the sky the width of three full moons. In a very dark sky, it appears as a blurry patch or misty cloud to the naked eye. With binoculars or small telescopes, it's possible to see many stars shining out from a blurry background. The Romans called it Praesepe, which means "manger" or "crib." To astronomers, it is known as Messier 44, or M44 for short.

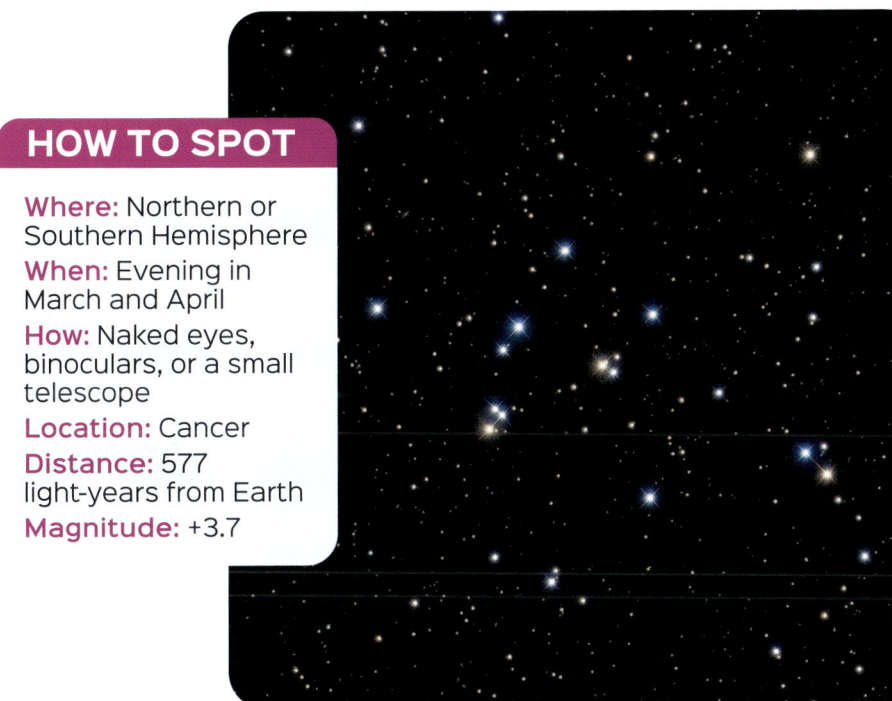

HOW TO SPOT

Where: Northern or Southern Hemisphere

When: Evening in March and April

How: Naked eyes, binoculars, or a small telescope

Location: Cancer

Distance: 577 light-years from Earth

Magnitude: +3.7

MESSIER OBJECTS

In the 1700s, astronomer Charles Messier mistook the Crab Nebula for a comet. He wanted to make it easier for others to avoid such mistakes in the future. He cataloged 110 star clusters, nebulae, and galaxies in the Northern Hemisphere skies. These are still called Messier objects today. Each one is named with M plus a number.

STAR CLUSTERS

DOUBLE CLUSTER

Not many deep sky sights are visible to the naked eye, but the Double Cluster can be, especially when it rises high above the horizon in a very dark sky. Through binoculars, these clusters appear as twin masses of stars packed closely together. There are more than 300 supergiant stars in each cluster. These stars are all relatively young at around 12.8 million years old, and they are very hot. They shine with blue-white light. The clusters are separated from each other by just a few light-years. But they are about 7,500 light-years from Earth, located on a separate arm of the Milky Way galaxy.

HOW TO SPOT

Where: Northern Hemisphere
When: Best viewed in the evening in November and December
How: Naked eyes or binoculars
Location: Between Cassiopeia and Perseus
Distance: 7,500 light-years from Earth
Magnitude: +3.8

HERCULES GLOBULAR CLUSTER

The Hercules Globular Cluster is one of the most famous clusters in the northern sky. It contains as many as 300,000 stars and is 11.65 billion years old. It may be visible to the naked eye in a dark sky as a faint smudge. Through a telescope it looks like a pile of spilled salt. Every single "grain" is a star. The Hercules Globular Cluster's official name is Messier 13, or M13. It is located within the Keystone shape that marks the center of the constellation Hercules.

HOW TO SPOT

Where: Best viewed in the Northern Hemisphere
When: Evening in July and August
How: Binoculars
Location: Hercules
Distance: 22,200 light-years from Earth
Magnitude: +5.8

FUN FACT
The stars in this cluster are packed so closely together that they occasionally merge to form new stars.

The Hubble Space Telescope has spotted two colliding galaxies within the Hercules Globular Cluster.

STAR CLUSTERS

HYADES

The Hyades is the nearest star cluster to Earth and is fairly easy to see with the naked eye. Its V shape marks out the face of the constellation Taurus, which represents a bull. The bright star Aldebaran marks the bull's eye and one end of the V. Aldebaran is not actually a member of the cluster, though. It just appears nearby from Earth's perspective. The stars in the Hyades are relatively young and likely formed alongside the stars of the Beehive Cluster.

HOW TO SPOT

Where: Northern or Southern Hemisphere
When: Evening in January and February
How: Naked eyes
Location: Taurus
Distance: 153 light-years from Earth
Magnitude: +0.5

FUN FACT
The Milky Way's gravity is tearing stars away from the Hyades, forming two tails that are hundreds of light-years long.

JEWEL BOX

The Jewel Box is a cluster that got its name when astronomer John Herschel compared it to fancy jewelry. Usually, the stars in one cluster are all the same type and color. But the stars of the Jewel Box cluster are different and shine in varying shades of red, yellow, and blue, resembling gems. The Jewel Box is visible only in the Southern Hemisphere. It can be found in the constellation Crux, the Southern Cross. To the naked eye, the Jewel Box appears as a fuzzy star. The colors become visible in large binoculars or telescopes. The Jewel Box is around 14 million years old, which is very young for a star cluster.

HOW TO SPOT

Where: Southern Hemisphere
When: Best viewed in the evening in May
How: Naked eyes
Location: Crux
Distance: 6,440 light-years from Earth
Magnitude: +4.2

The Jewel Box cluster through a telescope

STAR CLUSTERS

OMEGA CENTAURI GLOBULAR CLUSTER

Omega Centauri, home to a whopping 10 million stars, is the largest star cluster in the Milky Way. It is ten times larger than a typical globular cluster. The stars are packed very closely together. Strangely, the stars in this cluster did not form all at once. Some scientists think this cluster is all that's left of a small galaxy that got absorbed into the Milky Way. In the Southern Hemisphere, Omega Centauri looks like a fuzzy glowing spot to the naked eye. A telescope brings a colorful swarm of stars into view.

HOW TO SPOT

Where: Southern Hemisphere
When: Best viewed in the evening in April and May
How: Naked eyes
Location: Centaurus
Distance: 15,600 light-years from Earth
Magnitude: +5.3

PLEIADES

The Pleiades, also known as the Seven Sisters, is one of the most famous sights in the entire night sky. Even in an area with some light pollution, five of the seven brightest stars should be easy to find. A line from Orion's belt through the star Aldebaran leads to the Pleiades. They form the same shape as the Big Dipper but much, much tinier. Binoculars or telescopes will reveal even more stars—the cluster contains around 3,000 of them. Many different cultures worldwide have told stories about the Pleiades. In Greek mythology, they were the seven daughters of Atlas, the giant who held the world on his shoulders.

HOW TO SPOT

Where: Northern or Southern Hemisphere
When: Evening in January and February
How: Naked eyes
Location: Taurus
Distance: 444 light-years from Earth
Magnitude: +2.9 to +4.2

FUN FACT
The Inuit of Greenland have seen the Pleiades as a pack of dogs hunting a polar bear.

NEBULAE

CARINA NEBULA

The Carina Nebula is one of the largest and brightest nebulae in the sky, but it is visible only from the Southern Hemisphere. From a very dark location on a clear night, it appears to the naked eye as a faint, fuzzy cloud a bit larger than the full moon surrounding the star Eta Carinae. This star is dying, but in other parts of the nebula new stars are being born. Binoculars can reveal interesting shapes and structures inside the nebula. Professional space photographs reveal the nebula's stunning pink and red colors.

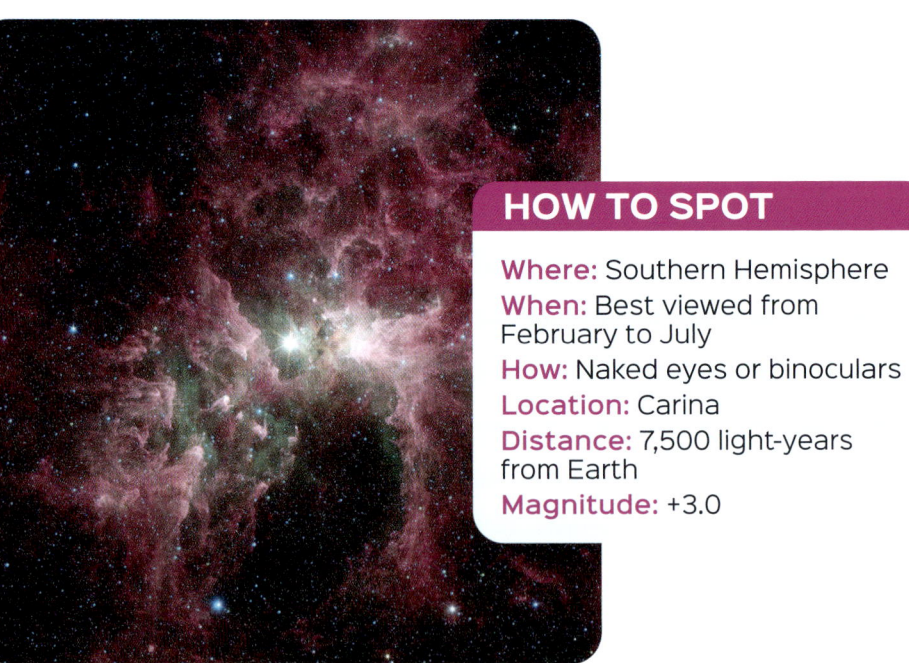

HOW TO SPOT

Where: Southern Hemisphere
When: Best viewed from February to July
How: Naked eyes or binoculars
Location: Carina
Distance: 7,500 light-years from Earth
Magnitude: +3.0

WHAT IS A NEBULA?

A nebula is a like a gigantic cloud in outer space. A nebula contains dust and gas spread out over an area many light-years across. Some are places where new stars are born. Others are the remnants left after a star has exploded. Some glow with light or brilliant colors. Others are dark and block light.

COALSACK NEBULA

The Coalsack Nebula got its name because it is as dark as coal. It is a vast cloud made of cold gas and dust that blocks out almost all the light from stars behind it. Any light that does make it through appears reddish. To the naked eye, the Coalsack Nebula looks like an oddly empty patch of sky in the midst of the Milky Way, right next to the constellation Crux. The Coalsack Nebula won't remain dark forever. In several million years, the dust and gas will come together to form stars.

HOW TO SPOT

Where: Southern Hemisphere
When: Best viewed in the evening in May
How: Naked eyes
Location: Crux
Type: Dark nebula
Distance: 600 light-years from Earth
Magnitude: Dark

A photo taken by an astronaut on the International Space Station shows the Coalsack Nebula in the bottom left.

FUN FACT
The Coalsack Nebula forms the head of the Emu in the Sky, a constellation from Australian Aboriginal cultures.

NEBULAE

CRAB NEBULA

In the year 1054, astronomers in China, Arabia, and elsewhere noticed that a new, very bright star had appeared in the sky. Scientists today know it was a supernova, an exploding star. The explosion left behind a cloud of dust and gas that has been expanding ever since. This is the Crab Nebula, also called M1. The nebula got its name from an early drawing that made it look crab-like. Through a backyard telescope, it looks more like a blurry oval. Professional photographs of the nebula reveal brilliant red and blue colors.

HOW TO SPOT

Where: Northern or Southern Hemisphere
When: Evening in January and February
How: Telescope
Location: Taurus
Type: Supernova remnant
Distance: 6,500 light-years from Earth
Magnitude: +8.4

FUN FACT
The supernova that created the Crab Nebula was so bright it was visible in the daytime sky for almost a month in 1054.

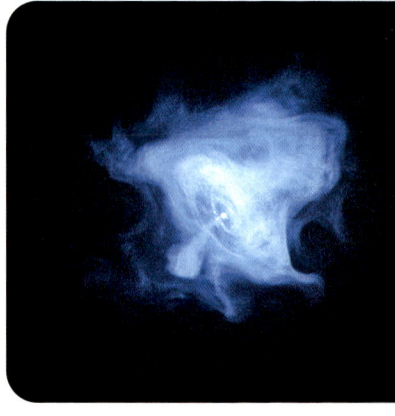

Images from X-ray telescopes reveal different shapes inside the Crab Nebula.

DUMBBELL NEBULA

The Dumbbell Nebula, or M27, got its name because it looks a bit like a weight people use for exercising. It also resembles an apple core or hourglass. It was the first planetary nebula ever discovered. This type of nebula actually has nothing to do with planets. It is the remnants of a star that ran out of fuel and collapsed. Our sun will eventually become this type of nebula. The Dumbbell Nebula is located inside the Southern Triangle between Vulpecula (the Fox) and Sagitta (an arrow).

HOW TO SPOT

Where: Best viewed in the Northern Hemisphere
When: Evening in September
How: Telescope
Location: Between Vulpecula and Sagitta
Type: Planetary nebula
Distance: 1,400 light-years from Earth
Magnitude: +7.4

NEBULAE
EAGLE NEBULA

One of the most well-known images of outer space shows the Eagle Nebula, or M16. The Hubble Space Telescope took the picture in 1995. It shows only the very center of the nebula. Dark, towering, cloud-like forms made of dust rise like pillars. Inside, stars are being born. The photo is named *The Pillars of Creation*. Through a typical telescope, the Eagle Nebula looks like a misty cloud sprinkled with bright stars. These newly formed stars are 6 million years old or younger. This nebula is located between the teapot shape in Sagittarius and the tail end of the constellation Serpens.

HOW TO SPOT

Where: Northern or Southern Hemisphere

When: Evening in June and July

How: Telescope

Location: Between Sagittarius and Serpens

Distance: 7,000 light-years from Earth

Magnitude: +6.0

FUN FACT
The sun likely formed inside a nebula similar to the Eagle Nebula.

HORSEHEAD NEBULA

The Horsehead Nebula, a dark cloud that looks like a horse or seahorse's head, may be even more famous than the Eagle Nebula. However, it's much more difficult to spot through a backyard telescope. The good news is that it's just one small part of a vast area of amazing deep sky sights, the Orion Molecular Cloud Complex. This area takes up most of the sky around the constellation Orion. The Horsehead Nebula and its neighbor, the Flame Nebula, are located next to Alnitak, the lowest star in Orion's belt. Stars are being formed inside both of these nebulae.

HOW TO SPOT

Where: Northern or Southern Hemisphere
When: Evening in January and February
How: Large telescope
Location: Orion
Distance: 1,400 light-years from Earth
Magnitude: Dark

NEBULAE

ORION NEBULA

Just below Orion's distinctive belt, there is a line of three faint stars, usually called Orion's sword. The middle star isn't actually a star at all. It's the Orion Nebula, or M42, one of the only nebulae bright enough to see with the naked eye. It looks like a slightly fuzzy star. It is actually 20,000 times larger than our solar system. New stars are being formed in the nebula. Through a telescope, billowing cloudy shapes and a sprinkle of baby stars become visible. Professional space photography equipment captures the brilliant green and red colors of this star nursery.

FUN FACT

The ancient Maya of South America saw the belt and feet of Orion as a hearth. The Orion Nebula was known as the Fire of Creation.

HOW TO SPOT

Where: Northern or Southern Hemisphere
When: Evening in January and February
How: Naked eyes or binoculars
Location: Orion
Distance: 1,300 light-years from Earth
Magnitude: +4.0

RING NEBULA

The Ring Nebula reveals what happens soon after a star the size of the sun dies. The nebula, also called M57, looks like a donut lit up from the center. The donut shape is a cloud of expanding gas. A white dwarf, all that is left of the star, sits at the center. A backyard telescope can pick up the distinctive ring shape of this nebula, which will appear silvery grey. However, professional space photographs reveal a rainbow of blue, yellow, green, and red extending outward from the middle of the ring.

HOW TO SPOT

Where: Best viewed in the Northern Hemisphere
When: Evening in July and August
How: Telescope
Location: Lyra
Distance: 2,300 light-years from Earth
Magnitude: +8.8

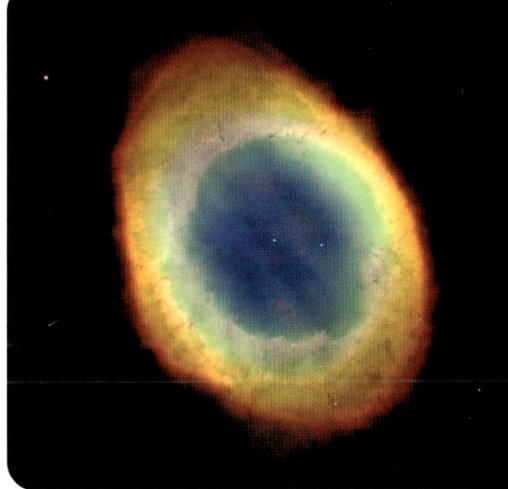

The Ring Nebula from the Hubble Space Telescope

The Ring Nebula through a backyard telescope

GALAXIES

ANDROMEDA GALAXY

The Andromeda Galaxy, officially named M31, is the most distant object that can be seen with the naked eye. It can be seen only in a dark, clear sky. It looks like a fuzzy blur wider than the full moon and slightly oval in shape. Early astronomers thought it was a nebula inside the Milky Way. Then, in 1925, Edwin Hubble proved that it was so far away it had to be a separate galaxy. It is the closest large spiral galaxy to the Milky Way and moving closer. The two galaxies will eventually collide with each other, but not for another 4 billion years or so.

HOW TO SPOT

Where: Best viewed from the Northern Hemisphere
When: Evening in November
How: Naked eyes
Location: Between Cassiopeia and Pegasus
Distance: 2.5 million light-years from Earth
Magnitude: +3.4

LARGE AND SMALL MAGELLANIC CLOUDS

The Large and Small Magellanic Clouds are dwarf spiral galaxies that orbit the Milky Way. They are visible only from the Southern Hemisphere, appearing as cloudy patches in the sky near the point that all the southern constellations rotate around. In some parts of South America, people called them feathers of a rhea, an ostrich-like bird. In an Australian Aboriginal tale, the two clouds are an old man and woman.

HOW TO SPOT

Where: Southern Hemisphere
When: All year
How: Naked eyes
Location: Opposite from Crux, near the south celestial pole
Distance: 163,000 light-years (large) and 200,000 light-years (small) from Earth
Magnitude: +0.9 (large) and +2.7 (small)

The Large Magellanic Cloud

The Small Magellanic Cloud

FUN FACT
There is a North Star, but no South Star. The southern constellations rotate around a dark patch of sky.

GALAXIES

THE MILKY WAY

The Milky Way is where Earth is located. The galaxy is shaped like a gigantic, flat disk with a black hole in the center and long, curving, spiral arms. The sun rotates around the center of the galaxy in a small arm called the Orion arm. From Earth, the galaxy appears as a band of cloudy light stretching across the entire sky. Unfortunately, even a small amount of light pollution hides the Milky Way from view. A very dark sky is required to see it. The Milky Way got its name from a Greek myth in which the goddess Hera spills milk across the sky.

FUN FACT
Some cultures named dark patches within the Milky Way. The Incas saw a llama and a serpent, while the Māori of New Zealand saw a shark.

HOW TO SPOT

Where: Anywhere with a very dark sky
When: All year, but best viewed in July and August
How: Naked eyes
Location: Stretching across the entire sky
Magnitude: Varies

WHIRLPOOL GALAXY

The Whirlpool Galaxy, also known as M51, is one of the most incredible sights to see with a telescope. It faces toward Earth, showing off its entire spiraling shape. This galaxy can be found near the last star in the handle of the Big Dipper, part of Ursa Major. A large enough telescope will reveal a smaller galaxy right next to this one. The Whirlpool Galaxy is slowly absorbing the smaller galaxy.

HOW TO SPOT

Where: Northern Hemisphere
When: Evening in May
How: Telescope
Location: Near the Big Dipper
Distance: 23 million light-years from Earth
Magnitude: +8.4

The Whirlpool Galaxy from the NuSTAR space telescope

The Whirlpool Galaxy through a backyard telescope

COMETS

HALLEY'S COMET

Comets are often described as dirty snowballs because they are made mainly of ice, rock, and dust. As they approach the hot sun, comets grow long tails of glowing dust and gas. Halley's Comet is the most famous one because it returns about every 75 years and can be seen with the naked eye when it arrives. Throughout history, many people have noted its arrival. Astronomer Edmond Halley was the first to realize these sightings were connected.

HOW TO SPOT

Where: Northern or Southern Hemisphere
When: Most recently came near Earth in 1986; will return in 2061
How: Naked eyes

A European spacecraft studied Halley's Comet up close in 1986.

FUN FACT

A comet may have smashed into Earth about 66 million years ago, leading to the extinction of the dinosaurs.

FUTURE BRIGHT COMETS

Comets are tricky to predict. Most comets that zip past Earth are too small and dim to see without a telescope. For a comet to appear very brightly and clearly, a lot of things have to line up just right, including the comet's orbit, Earth's orbit, the comet's composition, and more. The news and social media will get the word out when a bright comet is approaching. A few to watch out for include Hartley 2, PanSTARRS, and Pons-Brooks. Some comets stick around in the sky for a while. The comet Hale-Bopp was visible for 18 months in 1996 and 1997. It won't return for more than 2,000 years, though.

HOW TO SPOT

Where: Check online for news
When: Check online for news
How: Naked eyes

The comet NEOWISE appeared in the night sky in 2020. It will return in about 6,800 years.

HOW DOES A COMET FORM?

Some comets come from the Oort Cloud, a gigantic shell made of trillions of icy objects. This shell surrounds the solar system. Sometimes an object gets knocked out of the shell and moves toward the sun. The sun's heat causes gas and dust to stream away in a glowing tail. Other comets come from the Kuiper Belt, a collection of icy objects that orbit the sun past the planet Neptune.

METEOR SHOWERS

QUADRANTIDS

During a meteor shower, streaks of light regularly appear in the sky. People call them shooting stars, but they are not stars. They are bits of ice and dust vaporizing in the atmosphere, shining with heat and light. Single meteors may fall at any time of the year. But when Earth passes through a field of debris, usually left behind by a comet, many fall at once. This is a meteor shower. The Quadrantid meteor shower has fireball meteors that shine more brightly and last longer in the sky than typical meteors. However, this shower usually lasts for just a few hours on one night of the year.

HOW TO SPOT

Where: Northern Hemisphere
When: December or January; check NASA's website for the specific date and time
Meteors per hour: 60 to 200
How: Naked eyes
Location: In the area around Boötes

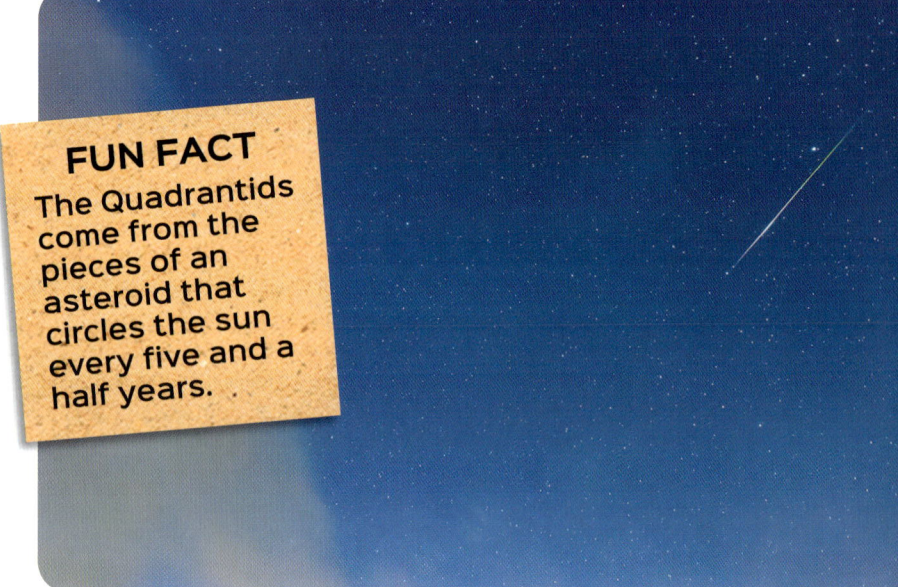

FUN FACT
The Quadrantids come from the pieces of an asteroid that circles the sun every five and a half years.

PERSEIDS

The Perseids is one of the most popular meteor showers to watch in the Northern Hemisphere. It has a high rate of meteors and happens in midsummer when the temperatures outside at night are pleasant. The debris for this shower comes from a comet named Swift-Tuttle, which swings nearby every 130 years. In China and Japan, there is a famous story about lovers represented by the stars Altair and Vega. They are separated by the Milky Way, and they reunite once a year. If they are unable to meet that day, the woman cries. Some say the Perseids represent her tears.

Time-lapse images show multiple meteors at once.

HOW TO SPOT

Where: Northern Hemisphere
When: July or August; check NASA's website for the specific date and time
Meteors per hour: Up to 100
How: Naked eyes
Location: Across the entire sky

HOW TO WATCH A METEOR SHOWER

The peak of a meteor shower doesn't last very long. A clear and moonless night and an area well away from any light pollution are best for viewing. At the correct time, hopeful viewers should lie down outside on a blanket, look up, and wait for meteors to fall. Patience is key.

METEOR SHOWERS

LEONIDS

On November 13, 1833, people around the United States witnessed a night sky filled with shining meteors. It was the Leonids, but it wasn't a typical meteor shower. It was a meteor storm! Throughout the night, 50,000 to 150,000 meteors fell every hour. A similar storm happened in 1966. The Leonids may storm like this whenever their parent comet, Tempel-Tuttle, passes close to the sun. This happens every 33 years. The next chance to witness a sky filled with Leonid meteors will come in 2031.

HOW TO SPOT

Where: Northern or Southern Hemisphere

When: November; check NASA's website for the specific date and time

Meteors per hour: Usually around 15

How: Naked eyes

Location: Across the entire sky

An illustration from the 1800s shows Earth crossing the path of meteoroids that make up the Leonids.

GEMINIDS

Many consider the Geminids to be the best meteor shower of the year. The meteors move at about half the speed of those in a Leonid or Perseid shower. Instead of flashing by in the blink of an eye, each one shines for a few seconds and may follow a jagged path. These meteors may appear tinted yellow, red, orange, blue, or even green. An asteroid named 3200 Phaethon is the source of the debris for this shower. It's a very unusual asteroid because it is colored blue and has a tail like a comet.

HOW TO SPOT

Where: Best viewed in the Northern Hemisphere
When: December; check NASA's website for the specific date and time
Meteors per hour: Around 50
How: Naked eyes
Location: Gemini

FUN FACT
The Eta Aquarids in May is considered to be the best meteor shower of the year in the Southern Hemisphere.

ATMOSPHERIC PHENOMENA

THE NORTHERN AND SOUTHERN LIGHTS

In the most northern and southern parts of planet Earth, colorful sheets of light occasionally dance across the night sky. The technical names for them are aurora borealis in the north and aurora australis in the south. Most people know them as the northern and southern lights. They happen when the sun sends out streams of charged particles called solar wind. Earth's magnetic field deflects solar wind toward the poles. When enough particles hit gases in the atmosphere, the sky lights up.

HOW TO SPOT

Where: Near the Arctic or Antarctica
When: Best viewed during March or September
How: Naked eyes
Location: Near the horizon in the direction of the closest pole

FUN FACT
Many cultures have associated the northern lights with ghosts or the spirits of people who have died.

Astronauts can see auroras from space.

SPRITES

Sprites are bursts of electricity similar to lightning strikes. But sprites never come near the ground. They look sort of like red jellyfish that appear high in the sky for a brief moment. For years, scientists thought sprites were a myth. But in 1989, a pilot took a video of them. They don't come from the same storm clouds as rain and regular lightning. They happen in the very top layer of the atmosphere, a region called the mesosphere. Though they look small from the ground, they can be 30 miles (48 km) wide.

HOW TO SPOT

Where: Best viewed in the Midwestern United States
When: During a thunderstorm at night
How: Naked eyes
Location: High in the sky

HUMAN OBJECTS

INTERNATIONAL SPACE STATION

The International Space Station (ISS) looks like a rapidly moving bright star. In fact, it can shine as brightly as the planet Venus in the sky. It is easy to see, but viewing it requires some planning. The ISS moves so quickly that it takes just two to four minutes for it to zip across the sky from the eastern horizon to the western horizon. It will make several passes in one night, though, and it will be visible during the night in any given area for several weeks. Several people are inside the ISS at all times.

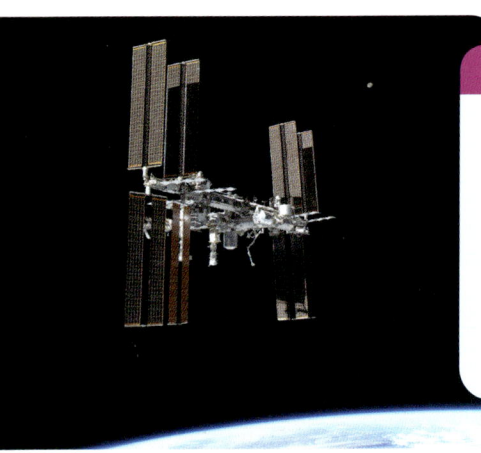

HOW TO SPOT

Where: Northern or Southern Hemisphere
When: Check online at the NASA website Spot the Station
How: Naked eyes
Altitude: 280 miles (451 km) above Earth
Magnitude: As bright as -3.9

From the ground, the ISS can be seen zooming across the night sky.

SATELLITES

Satellites are machines that orbit Earth. Some track weather, some take pictures, and some assist with communications. As of 2021, more than 4,000 active satellites orbited the planet. That number is only going to grow in the future. Companies are planning to launch thousands of satellites that will beam internet connections to people on the ground. Seeing satellites is easy. On a clear night, most people can see one approximately every 15 minutes. It looks like a speck of white light moving steadily in a line across the sky. However, if the light has flashing or colored lights, it's an airplane.

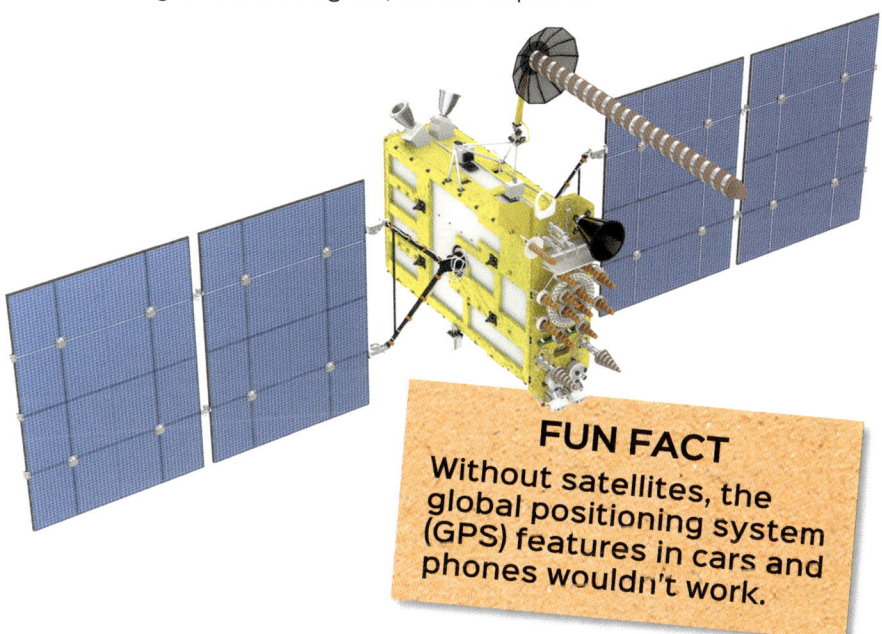

FUN FACT
Without satellites, the global positioning system (GPS) features in cars and phones wouldn't work.

HOW TO SPOT

Where: Northern or Southern Hemisphere
When: Anytime
How: Naked eyes
Altitude: Most are between 100 and 1,200 miles (161 and 1,930 km) above Earth
Magnitude: Varies

GLOSSARY

asteroid
A rocky object that orbits the sun but isn't large enough to be a planet.

astronomer
A person who studies outer space.

atmosphere
The gases surrounding a planet.

axis
The line that a planet, moon, or other object rotates around.

crater
A bowl-like hole left on the surface of a planet or moon after an object strikes it.

distinctive
A quality that sets something apart or helps identify it.

equator
The line that separates the northern and southern halves of Earth.

hemisphere
One half of a planet or sphere.

immortal
Lasting forever or unable to die.

meteor
An object from space that vaporizes in Earth's sky. Also called a shooting star.

mythology
A group of stories that all belong to one culture.

nebula
A massive, cloud-like collection of dust and gas in outer space.

orbit
The path an object such as a planet or moon follows around a separate object.

TO LEARN MORE

FURTHER READINGS

Oseid, Kelsey. *What We See in the Stars: An Illustrated Tour of the Night Sky*. Ten Speed Press, 2017.

Read, John A. *50 Things to See with a Telescope*. Stellar Publishing, 2018.

Thacher, Meg. *Sky Gazing*. Storey Publishing, 2020.

ONLINE RESOURCES

To learn more about the night sky, please visit **abdobooklinks.com** or scan this QR code. These links are routinely monitored and updated to provide the most current information available.

PHOTO CREDITS

Cover Photos: iStockphoto, front (Saturn), front (moon), front (aurora); Shutterstock Images, front (asteroid), front (meteor shower), front (nebula), back (Mars), back (Jupiter); JSC/NASA, front (space station); Red Line Editorial, front (big dipper), back (Orion); JPL-Caltech/NASA, front (galaxy); Denis Belitsky/Shutterstock Images, front (milky way); Yurij Omelchenko/Shutterstock Images, back (satellite)

Interior Photos: Shutterstock Images, 4 (Neptune), 4 (Leo), 5 (Libra), 5 (satellite), 5 (Scorpio), 5 (Venus), 8 (bottom), 13, 15 (top), 15 (bottom), 16 (left), 17, 18 (top), 20 (bottom), 21, 23, 24 (top), 26 (top), 26 (bottom), 27, 28, 30, 31 (top), 31 (bottom), 32, 33 (top), 34, 35 (top), 36, 37 (top), 38 (bottom), 39 (top), 39 (bottom), 40, 41 (top), 41 (bottom), 42, 43 (bottom), 44, 45 (top), 46, 47 (bottom), 48 (top), 49, 50 (right), 51, 52, 53 (bottom), 55, 56 (top), 57, 58 (top), 58 (bottom), 65 (bottom), 66 (top), 67, 68, 69, 71 (bottom), 74 (bottom), 78, 79, 80, 81 (top), 82, 83 (bottom), 96, 107, 112 (Venus), 112 (satellite), 112 (Callisto), 112 (stargazer);

iStockphoto, 4 (meteorite), 29 (bottom), 59; Aleksandr Morrisovich/Shutterstock Images, 4 (moon), 22 (top); Pavel Chagochkin/Shutterstock Images, 5 (asteroids), 112 (asteroids); Johns Hopkins University Applied Physics Laboratory/Carnegie Institution of Washington/NASA, 8 (top); JPL/NASA, 9, 20 (top); JPL/USGS/NASA, 10; JPL-Caltech/UCLA/MPS/DLR/IDA/NASA, 11 (right), 12 (top), 12 (bottom); JPL-Caltech/NASA, 11 (left), 85, 86, 94; Vadim Sadovski/Shutterstock Images, 14; MSFC/NASA, 16 (right); JSC/NASA, 18 (bottom), 87 (bottom), 104 (bottom), 106 (top); Harm Kruyshaar/Shutterstock Images, 19; David Hajnal/Shutterstock Images, 22 (bottom), 97 (bottom); KSC/NASA, 24 (bottom); JPL/JHUAPL/NASA, 25; Digital Storm/Shutterstock Images, 29 (top); Natalia Hubbert/Shutterstock Images, 33 (bottom), 54 (bottom); Massimo Todaro/Shutterstock Images, 35 (bottom); Nastya Moon/Shutterstock Images, 37 (bottom); Alexandr Yurtchenko/iStockphoto, 43 (top); Hoika Mikhail/Shutterstock Images, 45 (bottom); Roman Voloshyn/Shutterstock Images, 47 (top);

Juan Aunion/Shutterstock Images, 48 (bottom); Morphart Creation/Shutterstock Images, 50 (left); Vera Shestak/iStockphoto, 53 (top); Dorota Janus/Shutterstock Images, 54 (top); Alberto Clemares Exposito/Shutterstock Images, 56 (bottom); Tragoolchitr Jittasaiyapan/Shutterstock Images, 60, 61 (top), 62 (bottom), 63, 65 (top), 77; M. Kornmesser/ESO, 61 (bottom); K. Ohnaka/ESO, 62 (top); Cristian Cestaro/Shutterstock Images, 64, 72 (top); Mullard Radio Astronomy Laboratory/Science Source, 66 (bottom); Davide De Martin/ESA/Hubble/NASA, 70; Nitish Waila/Shutterstock Images, 72; Neven Krcmarek/Shutterstock Images, 73; John Chumack/Science Source, 74 (top); Genevieve de Messieres/Shutterstock Images, 75, 103; QA International/Science Source, 76; K. Noll/Hubble Collaboration/AURA-ESA/NASA, 81 (bottom); Brian Donovan/Shutterstock Images, 83 (top), 98 (top); JPL-Caltech/NOAO/AURA/NSF/NASA, 84; Rev. Ronald Royer/Science Source, 87 (top); ESA/JPL/Arizona State University/NASA, 88 (top); NASA Goddard/NASA, 88 (bottom); JPL-Caltech/Harvard-Smithsonian CfA/NASA, 89; STScI/AURA/NASA, 90 (top); JPL-Caltech/Institut d'Astrophysique Spatiale/NASA, 90 (bottom); STScI/ESA/NASA, 91; JPL-Caltech/UCLA/NASA, 92; JPL-Caltech/ESA/Hubble Heritage Team/STScI/AURA/NASA, 93 (top); Albert Barr/Shutterstock Images, 93 (bottom); JPL-Caltech/STScI/NASA, 95 (top), 95 (bottom); JPL-Caltech/IPAC/NASA, 97 (top); Giotto Project/ESA/NASA, 98 (bottom); Mark A. Lee/Shutterstock Images, 99; Ben Pong/Shutterstock Images, 100; NASA/Science Source, 101; Science Source, 102 (right); SPL/Science Source, 102 (left); John A Davis/Shutterstock Images, 104 (top); ESO/Petr Horalek/Science Source, 105; Sergey Kamshylin/Shutterstock Images, 106 (bottom)

ABDOBOOKS.COM

Published by Abdo Publishing, a division of ABDO, PO Box 398166, Minneapolis, Minnesota 55439. Copyright © 2022 by Abdo Consulting Group, Inc. International copyrights reserved in all countries. No part of this book may be reproduced in any form without written permission from the publisher. Abdo Reference™ is a trademark and logo of Abdo Publishing.

Printed in the United States of America, North Mankato, Minnesota.
102021
012022

THIS BOOK CONTAINS RECYCLED MATERIALS

Editor: Arnold Ringstad
Series Designer: Colleen McLaren
Content Consultant: Dr. Douglas Duncan; Department of Astrophysical & Planetary Sciences; University of Colorado

Library of Congress Control Number: 2021941707
Publisher's Cataloging-in-Publication Data
Names: Hulick, Kathryn, author.
Title: The night sky / by Kathryn Hulick
Description: Minneapolis, Minnesota : Abdo Publishing, 2022 |
    Series: Field guides for kids | Includes online resources and index.
Identifiers: ISBN 9781532196980 (lib. bdg.) | ISBN 9781098218799
    (ebook)
Subjects: LCSH: Sky--Juvenile literature. | Astronomy--Juvenile
    literature. | Moon--Juvenile literature. | Stars--Juvenile literature. |
    Field guides--Juvenile literature.
Classification: DDC 520--dc23

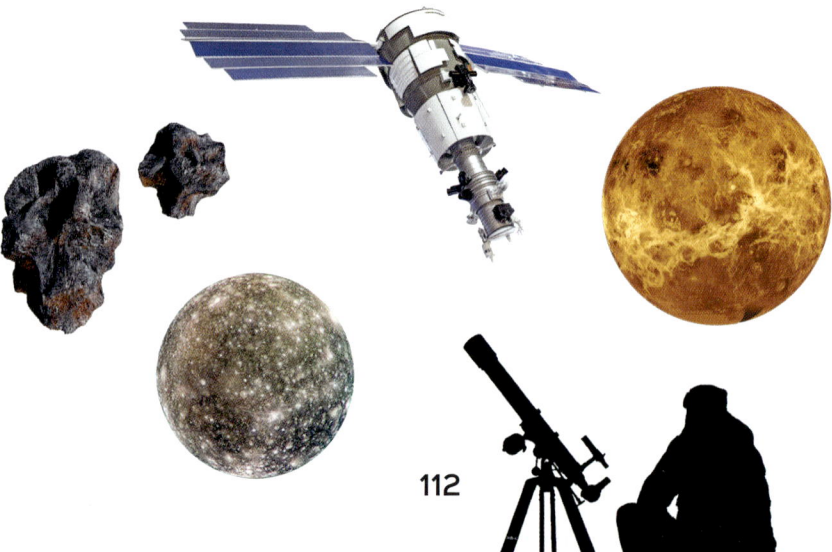